FIVE NICKELS

Also by Jim "Boots" Demarest

Joint Force Leadership:
How SEALs and Fighter Pilots Lead to Success

FIVE NICKELS

TRUE STORY OF THE
DESERT STORM HEROICS AND SACRIFICE OF
AIR FORCE CAPTAIN STEVE PHILLIS

JIM "BOOTS" DEMAREST

PERMUTED
PRESS

A PERMUTED PRESS BOOK

Five Nickels:
True Story of the Desert Storm Heroics and Sacrifice
of Air Force Captain Steve Phillis
© 2022 by Jim "Boots" Demarest
All Rights Reserved

ISBN: 978-1-63758-259-6
ISBN (eBook): 978-1-63758-260-2

Interior design and composition by Greg Johnson, Textbook Perfect

PERMUTED
PRESS

Permuted Press, LLC
New York • Nashville
permutedpress.com

Published in the United States of America
2 3 4 5 6 7 8 9 10

To Gabriela and Chad,
So that you will know a true hero when you see one.

To Karysia,
Forever my hero.

Contents

Prologue: The Shootdown 1

Part 1: The Strong-Willed Child 7

Part 2: The Academy 12

Part 3: The Real Air Force 25

Part 4: The Mighty Hog 45

Part 5: Alex 55

Part 6: Suwon 65

Part 7: The Beach 77

Part 8: The Desert 99

Part 9: The Storm 144

Part 10: The Search 172

Part 11: The Real Story 194

Bibliography 219

Acknowledgments 223

About the Author 225

The Shootdown

Captain Steve Phillis launched on his thirtieth combat mission of Operation Desert Storm on February 15, 1991. A highly experienced Air Force A-10 fighter pilot, Steve was leading his two-ship formation, call sign "Enfield 3-7," on their most challenging mission of the war—attacking Saddam Hussein's elite Medina Division of the Republican Guard. The Medina were dug in one hundred miles north of the border between Saudi Arabia and Kuwait, and they were equipped with Iraq's most modern air-defense equipment. It was tough tasking, but Steve and his wingman were quietly confident in their ability to get the job done.

Steve's wingman was First Lieutenant Rob Sweet, a young A-10 pilot who had grown up fast during Desert Storm and showed talent well beyond his years and experience. Rob and Steve flew as a combat pair during the war, and both had experience being shot at by Iraqi forces. To thrive and survive, each pilot had specific mission responsibilities. Steve's duties as flight lead were clear—drop bombs on target and bring both aircraft safely back to base. Rob's job as wingman was to follow Steve's lead and support his efforts to get both of them back home safely. After a month of combat flying, both understood the risks they would face.

The Medina Division endured regular aerial bombing by a host of coalition attack aircraft yet maintained an 85 percent combat effectiveness rating according to intelligence analysts. Over the preceding few days the air attacks had intensified, and February 15 was no exception. It was late in the afternoon when the Iraqi commander ordered several soldiers from his air defense company to man their Soviet built SA-13 Gopher/Strela-10 surface to-air missile (SAM) system mounted on a tracked armored vehicle. Most of the chassis was buried in the sand, leaving only the hatches, gunner's window, steerable turret, and missile canisters exposed.

They would get little notice of an attack. All the early warning radars were either destroyed or turned off to prevent engagement by a coalition aircraft. Any advance warning would arrive via information passed through a vast network of underground telephones, or as was more often the case, the crew simply relied on their eyes and ears to locate enemy aircraft. Several soldiers took up lookout positions around the SA-13 while the commander, gunner, and driver stood ready. All had clear orders: attack any coalition aircraft that strayed within the SA-13's three-mile range.

Enfield 3-7 flight entered the "kill box" occupied by the Medina Division. Steve and Rob took turns dropping bombs on military equipment and vehicles, with one attacking targets while the other watched out for SAM launches. They had seen several launches in the area and heard plenty of radio chatter from aircraft frantically maneuvering to prevent getting shot down. Their A-10s were well-equipped to defend against SAMs, but neither was eager to put these systems to use.

After several bombing passes, Steve noticed a truck traveling southwest on the only road in the area, so he and Rob followed. Steve rolled in and strafed the truck with the A-10's 30mm cannon but missed. The truck raced off the road and pulled into the center of a small circle of trucks parked on the south side. Rob rolled in and dropped cluster bombs on the truck park and covered about half the circle with bomblets. Steve called out that they had been in this target area long enough and directed the flight eastbound.

Through the smoke belching from burning vehicles and oil fires and the dust constantly kicked up by desert winds and coalition bombs, an Iraqi soldier spied two black dots approaching his position. Unable to initially identify these objects, of one thing he was sure. They were not Iraqi aircraft. He watched as the dots grew bigger and now suspected his unit was in for more trouble.

His fears were confirmed when the dots, now identified as aircraft, began to dive and drop bombs near his position. While not in the direct line of fire, he was close enough to see what was happening. His unit was being attacked from the air yet again. The initial attack was out of range of their SA-13s. However, after delivering their bombs, the aircraft circled back to attack a closer position. The commander ordered his team into their armored vehicle, and all three raced across the desert sand with an unmistakable sense of urgency.

The driver hopped into the open front-left hatch and reached over to start the engine. Once running, it would drive the internal generator used to power the entire weapons system. He reached up to close and lock the hatch behind him and turned on the generator. The system would be powered up in less than five seconds. Next in was the gunner, who scampered down the front-right hatch and moved quickly through the tight space back to his firing position. He unlocked the turret, placed his hands on the steering and fire controls, and began searching for the target through the blast-proof glass in front of him. The commander entered just behind the gunner, then reached up to close and lock the hatch. He confirmed both hatches and the window were locked, which was a requirement to launch. He put his headset on and activated the intercom, listening for words from his gunner.

The gunner looked down to confirm the COMBAT light was on steady and moved his thumbs over the push buttons atop the turret controls. He spun the turret to the south and continued looking for any coalition aircraft, eager to shoot one down with his "Arrow" missile. The Arrow was a seven-foot-long, eighty-six-pound missile designed to destroy high-performance aircraft at low altitude. The single-stage solid-propellant rocket motor boosted the missile to speeds in excess of twelve hundred miles per hour, and its thin white smoke trail was difficult to see from the air.

While flying eastbound, Steve spotted a lucrative target of riveted tanks in a three-mile-wide circle. There were no bomb craters anywhere in the formation, indicating that this unit had not come under recent attack in its present location. At first, Steve wondered whether he should even attack these targets, for fear that they were decoys. He decided to reposition the flight for what Rob believed to be their final attack, unaware of the flurry of activity going on below them.

The clear late afternoon sky provided perfect conditions and allowed the gunner to select this preferred targeting mode, optical tracking. High above his position, he spied a black dot slowly tracking across the sky and repositioned the launcher for a better look. He could not tell at first if it was an aircraft, but once he saw the unmistakable glow of a bright red flare in the late afternoon sky, he knew it was an aircraft, and a military aircraft at that.

The gunner watched as the aircraft drew closer, and he centered the target in the coarse sight, a mechanical reticle mounted near the top of his window. Once centered, he leaned forward and placed his head on the forehead pad to peer through the eyepiece. There, he found the crosshair used for visual aiming and located the target. He could make out the shape of a cross, which could only mean one thing. He was looking at a *bunduqiat samita*, a Silent Gun, the Iraqis' name for an American A-10 Warthog.

He pressed down on the button under his left thumb to command missile "boresight" mode. The fire control system sent a thirty-volt charge to the missile, which spun up gyros in the seeker head and readied it for target tracking. The gunner noted the BORESIGHT light on, heard the low-pitched beep in the headset meaning system ready, and looked down to find the tracking circle in his sight. He was able to smoothly track the slow-moving target circling overhead and centered it in his crosshairs.

Now he pressed down the button under his right thumb to the first stop to command missile tracking. The electromagnets holding the lid closed over missile number one energized to open, uncovering the seeker and allowing the missile to "look" for a target. The blue sky provided nice contrast for optical tracking of the dark silhouette, and as the gunner followed the target, he heard a low-pitched sound in his headset telling him missile number one was "seeing" the target.

The gunner centered his crosshairs over the A-10 and watched as the missile locked on and started tracking. The tone in his headset switched to a high-pitched sound, and he could see the tracking circle following the target through his field of view. Missile tracking confirmed, he kept the crosshairs over the target to ensure missile tracking at launch.

Before launching, the gunner had to ensure the target was within range, because the seeker could "see" the target long before the missile could reach it. The gunner used scale markings on the crosshairs, comparing them to the dimensions of the A-10 he'd memorized, concluded his target was below ten thousand feet, and well within the three-mile maximum engagement range of his Arrow.

Once in range and tracking, the gunner called "target capture" over the intercom, and the commander responded with, "Fire!" On command, the gunner pressed the TRACKING/FIRE button under his right thumb to the second stop and held it down. The fire control system shot an electrical charge to the missile, which set off an igniter to start the missile battery and quickly ready the missile for launch.

A second later, the on-board battery came up to voltage, and all missile systems were switched to internal power. In a split second, the missile confirmed launch requirements were met and sent a signal for rocket motor ignition. The missile erupted in a fury of smoke and flames as it exploded out of its canister. The crew heard the muffled blast and was momentarily blinded by the bright flash and cloud of white smoke from the rocket motor. The missile climbed skyward and tracked toward the target. It would only take seconds to get there.

The missile detonated just underneath the A-10's tail, and the warhead exploded with a flash of high-velocity shrapnel. Shrapnel penetrated the aircraft's skin, damaging or destroying anything in its path. Some effects were immediate, while others would take time to show themselves. Back on the ground, there were cheers followed by machine gun fire into the air in celebration. When black smoke was seen trailing behind the now-erratically flying Silent Gun, the missile crew knew for certain they had just made a contribution to Iraq's war effort. At the moment, it seemed like at least one of the A-10s in Enfield 3-7 flight would not make it back to base in time for dinner.

PART 1

The Strong-Willed Child

Stephen Richard Phillis

Doctor Richard "Bud" and Diane Phillis welcomed their first of five children, Stephen Richard, on May 17, 1960, at the Illinois Research and Educational Hospital in Chicago. Bud had just graduated from medical school and earned seventy-five dollars every two weeks as an intern, so adding a new mouth to feed was no small matter. Complicating life further was the fact that Steve was a very colicky baby who screamed day and night for the first six weeks of his life. While the screaming eventually stopped, the challenges of parenting him did not.

Steve was a stubborn and obstinate baby, the epitome of Dr. James Dobson's strong-willed child. Nothing was easy with young Steve, and everything Bud and Diane tried to do was met with some level of resistance. Long working hours afforded the young family little sleep, and although Bud and Diane knew Steve's strong will would serve him well one day, that day could not come soon enough.

When Steve was six years old, Bud was drafted into the Army but decided he wanted to go into the Air Force instead. In true

Phillis fashion, when he was unable to convince the local authorities about the wisdom of his way, he purchased an airline ticket and flew to Randolph Air Force Base to talk to the Surgeon General of the Air Force. After a fifteen minute conversation, Bud got assigned to the Air Force at F. E. Warren Air Force Base in Cheyenne, Wyoming and showed up weeks later as an Air Force doctor with no military training, just his usual crew cut and a set of orders.

Life in Cheyenne was great for the family, as Steve learned to ski and ride horses. But life out West was not without challenges. When Steve was in the first grade, he decided things were so bad at home that he needed to run away. He packed a lunch, along with several prized possessions, and ran away to live underneath the bleachers at the parade grounds, which, while in full view of the Phillis' home, was a long way for a first grader to go. After a few hours he returned home, and Diane later learned that when Steve heard that a friend of his was considering running away from home too, Steve told him not to do it, because it wouldn't be much fun.

Rock Island

Life as an Air Force doctor was simple, but Bud found it professionally unchallenging, so he was delighted to complete his required two-year tour then return home to Rock Island, Illinois. The Phillis family moved into a house large enough to hold Steve, his sister Cathy, and their younger brothers Mike, Tom, and Tim. They spent a lot of time together as a family and were regulars at the Sacred Heart Church.

Growing up, Steve's room was completely green, his favorite color. He had a collection of model airplanes and tanks that he built in excruciating detail, and he liked to play war with his brother Tom. Of course, older brother Steve would always win. Playing war did not involve guns, as they were not part of the Phillis household. Nor was fighting, which was absolutely not tolerated, so the kids never fought. There were, of course, disagreements, but they were never reduced to blows.

Steve didn't waste a lot of time trying to impress people. He was more of a quiet, confident kid. He was not the kind of person that sat around and chose his words carefully. He didn't have to. He knew what he wanted to say and just said it. He was the perfect fit for his Rock Island home and neighborhood.

Leading the Way

Steve was raised in a home with strong Catholic values. He served as an altar boy, as did his three brothers, and his love of music led him to join the church choir. His talents as a teacher emerged early when he was placed in charge of "altar boy classes," because he hated it when an altar boy stood up during the service and didn't know what to do. Steve's strong will evolved into strong leadership skills, and he was always up for a challenge. If a group needed a leader, he was the first to step forward and take charge.

The front yard of the Phillis house was the neighborhood playground. The kids were always playing some kind of team game, and Steve would always be a team captain. Everyone wanted to win, which meant that the same kids were always picked last, and Steve knew who was going to get picked last.

One day the kids decided to play a soccer game. All of the "good" athletes wanted to be on the same team, so Steve decided to captain the "other" team. He pulled them together, coached them up, and against all odds they won. His brother Tom said it best: "Steve just had this way of bringing out the best in people, and it didn't matter if you weren't good at something, or if you weren't athletic. Steve gave everyone else the opportunity to be better." Indeed, sports played a big part in Steve's life, but only if played the right way.

Steve was raised in a family where sportsmanship counted more than winning. If someone lost and got upset for losing, they were done for that day. Likewise, if they won, humility was the key. Rubbing a loss in somebody's face was simply not tolerated. Plain and simple, it was sportsmanship. Steve put this skill to the test as a high school football player, playing running back and defensive back. He was a good athlete, and in fact good at most things. He played trumpet, was a member of the National Honor Society, and ended up as the Senior Class Salutatorian.

A Calling

As high school graduation approached, Steve felt a calling to serve in the military—something that was not pushed in the Phillis household, nor was it frowned upon. Rather, Steve's parents gave him the gift of choice and helped him gather information about military service options.

Steve cast a wide net, competing for and earning Reserve Officer Training Corps (ROTC) scholarships from the Air Force and Navy, but his sights were set higher. Over a mile higher, in fact. Steve wanted to attend the United States Air Force Academy in Colorado Springs, Colorado.

The application process for the Air Force Academy was long and grueling, but Steve's dreams were best expressed in a letter dated September 20, 1977 he sent to Congressman Tom Railsback, seeking a nomination.

Dear Mr. Railsback,

It is my desire to attend the Air Force Academy and to serve in the United States Air Force. I respectfully request that I be considered as one of your nominees for the class that enters the Academy in June, 1978.

My reasons for wanting to enter the Air Force Academy are: I believe that every American has the duty to serve his country. I also believe in

discipline. At the Air Force Academy, I will not
only receive my education but will also be trained
in self-discipline that will be of value all
throughout my life.

I also enjoy physical activity and conditioning.
The Academy not only emphasizes mental exercise
but physical conditioning as well.

All throughout my life, I have wanted to learn
to fly jet aircraft. In the Air Force Academy, I
would not only be well trained as a pilot but also
be given ample opportunity to receive flying as a
great experience.

After months of waiting, Steve received a brief reply in the
mail from the Academy.

Dear Mr. Phillis,

I am pleased to offer you an appointment to the
U.S. Air Force Academy as a member of the class of
1982. This appointment is the first step toward a
challenging and rewarding career as a professional
Air Force officer. Congratulations.

Sincerely,

K.L. Tallman,
Lt. General, USAF
Superintendent

PART 2

The Academy

The Blue Zoo

In June of 1978, the Phillis family set out on a journey known to many—they were dropping off their oldest child at college. But this was no ordinary family trip to any ordinary college; it was a camping trip from Rock Island to Colorado Springs to deliver eldest child Steve to the United States Air Force Academy. The family piled into their station wagon laden with two weeks' worth of equipment and clothes, all of Steve's earthly possessions, and towing a camper. It was quite a sight.

The Phillis family left at four in the morning and planned to drive straight through each day with the only stops for gas. The kids were warned not to drink too much because dad would not tolerate any extra stops. Diane packed a huge cooler with sandwiches for lunch and had absolutely everything you could possibly want for snacks. Everyone knew the trip was a milestone for the family that not all were looking forward to. No one talked about Steve leaving, but it was on everyone's mind. Bud and Diane shared feelings of loss and uncertainty, particularly as they thought about Steve marching off into the unknown.

June 26 was a beautiful summer day in Colorado Springs, and the clear sky at seven thousand feet above sea level made the sun almost blinding. The Air Force Academy's modern architecture stood in stark contrast to the jagged mountains of the Rampart Range that rose in the northwestern corner of Colorado Springs. Known by some as the "Blue Zoo," the Academy's mission was to prepare young men and women of character to serve as officers in the United States Air Force.

The family car, still filled beyond capacity, was directed from the Academy's south gate through a series of winding roads which rose to the cadet area, Steve's destination. Steve was one of the 1,475 young men and women ordered to report for their first day of duty, and the scene was organized chaos. The Phillis family pulled up into the unloading zone where, after a brief goodbye, Steve was organized into a group with a dozen of his new classmates, all dressed in the fashions of the late '70s with hair to match. They were met by upper-class cadets wearing impeccably pressed uniforms and white gloves. The new cadets were lined up, taught how to stand at attention, and given a brief marching lesson. They then marched off into the uncertainty of the Academy, where their civilian identities were replaced with the uniforms of a basic cadet. The family would get one more chance to see Steve later that afternoon.

The swearing-in ceremony was held at the Cadet Field House, and the Phillis family arrived in plenty of time as instructed. Inside they found letters in alphabetical order taped to the backs of the seats, indicating where they might find their new cadet. The Field House was a sea of light blue shirts, dark blue pants and skirts, and mostly bald heads. After the swearing-in ceremony, the family finally found Steve with his head shaved and dressed like everybody else. It was a shock to everyone.

The family spent a few awkward moments finding out what Steve had just been through, but the truth was that everyone was coming to grips with something much more profound—the home in Rock Island would be without its oldest son from now on. Steve's sister and brother Tom cried at the thought, and his family watched him disappear into a mass of blue humanity when he was directed by an authoritative voice over the loudspeaker, "All basic cadets report to the cadet area." In a moment, both his civilian identity and youth were gone.

Beast

Basic Cadet Training, known as BCT or Beast, was the academy's program to transition teenage civilians into young military officer candidates. It was the Air Force Academy's version of boot camp, and with it came all that boot camp has to offer. Highly regimented days and nights, marching, drilling with rifles, physical fitness training, honor code training, marksmanship, assault course, and indoctrination into the academy's fourth-class system with its emphasis on discipline.

Beast was both a physical and mental challenge, and dozens of prospective members of the Class of 1982 left before Beast was over. This would be the first of many hurdles that Steve would have to clear in his four years at the academy.

His family knew that Steve was thriving in the pressure of the academy and had no doubt that he would graduate four years later, unless he decided to do something else. Dobson's strong-willed child was not about to let anything get in the way of his dreams. He did so well he was presented the Air Force Cadet Wing Outstanding Achievement award for superior performance in BCT. Good start.

Doolie Life

Freshmen at the Academy are called doolies, derived from the Greek word for slave. Doolie life was a seemly never-ending series of challenges. Academics, intramurals, inspections, parades, formations, football games, and military training filled every waking moment. Steve didn't love doolie life and got especially upset when a close friend of his dropped out of the Academy.

To cope, Steve starting dipping tobacco. An Academy friend got him started on Beech-Nut, and he went from there to Copenhagen, which he would dip for the rest of his life, and his mom hated it. Steve was not a casual dipper. He would put in a dip of Copenhagen in the morning and never spit. He would swallow the tobacco juice and keep a dip in all day and night. It was just something he did.

Steve struggled but managed to finish doolie year and was rewarded with a three-week summer training program called SERE, which stands for survival, evasion, resistance, and escape. Conducted in a remote part of the academy grounds, SERE taught survival techniques, including a prisoner of war (POW) environment.

The "resistance" portion subjected Steve to a controlled but realistic POW environment similar to that found by American POWs in Vietnam. Of course cadets were spared the extreme physical torture and traumas that actual POWs faced, but they were given a pretty healthy dose of uncomfortable situations as a test of both their ability to resist and their ability to function as a team. Although the resistance portion lasted two and a half days, it seemed like an eternity because of the sleep deprivation.

But there was one event that Steve and his classmates got to experience that would forever stand out in his mind. Late during the third day of captivity, the level of stress intensified to a crescendo. At that point, they had all the "prisoners" outside doing manual labor of some kind in a small, confined area. They were then forced to hide their faces in what was again supposed to be another reprimand from the camp commandant.

Instead, the "prisoners" were snapped to attention, given an about face command, and when they turned around, saw the American flag flying in the center of the compound as "The Star-Spangled Banner" blared from the loudspeaker system. It was a feeling Steve would never forget.

A Three-Hour Detour

Steve, like many cadets, took advantage of every opportunity to drive home for a visit. During one fateful trip, he spent a little too much time visiting his girlfriend and had to make up some time driving back. While racing his BMW 318 through Nebraska, he was pulled over by a state trooper for speeding. When Steve was unable to pay the eighty-dollar fine on the spot, he found himself in quite the jam.

Steve called home, and when his mother answered, he asked to speak to Dad. Dad was out making rounds, and although Steve tried to protect his mom, under the circumstances he had to tell her the truth. "Mom, my credit card is maxed, my checking account is overdrawn, and I don't have eighty dollars cash to pay the ticket." Then came the hard part: "I am being taken to the Lincoln County Jail to wait for the money."

What he failed to mention was that he had been locked up with a drunk and given a plate of plain beans for lunch. Steve's mom was frantic but calmed down enough to wire eighty dollars to the Western Union office located in the Tomahawk truck stop. Steve retrieved the money, paid the fine, and was released from jail after his three-hour detour. From that day forward, he would never again drive one mile an hour over the speed limit, no matter the circumstance. The experience changed his life, as did others in Colorado Springs.

The Airmanship Program

The Academy indeed provided Steve with an experience unlike any other college, and nowhere was that more true than in the airmanship program. The program included free-fall parachute jumping, soaring, and powered flight, and Steve got a taste of all three. First up was soaring, the most relaxed of them all.

Flying gliders in Colorado Springs was a thing of beauty. The Academy soaring program was supervised by officers but run by cadets, and all the instructors were cadets. This made for a formal but fun atmosphere. Soaring was Steve's first opportunity to fly something, and he was all in. He wrote a letter home on September 29, 1980 that captured his feelings.

Dear P-troop,

Now for the big news. Today I got a lot of flights in. The first flight I worked everything from take off to landing. The second flight, we were cruising up to altitude and Jim pulled the release and said 'simulated rope break'. I had to go through the procedures and I did okay.

The third flight was like the first, and the fourth and fifth were pattern tows where they take you just high enough to enter the pattern. This gave me the opportunity to practice my take off and landings.

When the fifth flight was over, we landed and Jim took off. He came back, went over some emergency procedures, and said 'you're cleared to solo!' I haven't had so many butterflies since I first asked a girl out.

I went through my checklist, waggled the rudder and off I went, solo. I cannot describe the feeling of flying, being in command and alone. I was totally on my own and I loved it. I flew a good pattern, landed well. Jim came running out, I opened the cockpit, he smiled and said "congratulations." It was excellent. We pulled the plane up to the runway and OIC said "this is the last tow," so I got to solo again.

I was still nervous, but I am at a loss for words. I am flying solo. I wish you could have seen me. After all those flights and activity, I was drained. Happy but drained. If things work out, I will get one, maybe two more solos this week.

Steve was hooked, and he got his second airmanship opportunity the following summer, only this time jumping out of perfectly good airplanes.

Steve volunteered to earn his military jump wings in the Academy's AM-490 free-fall parachute program. At the time, it was one of the few parachuting schools in the country where the jumper pulled his own ripcord on his first jump.

AM-490 students started in the classroom with a heavy emphasis on safety and were grilled daily on emergency procedures. Ground training included hands-on instruction with the equipment, aircraft exit, free-fall techniques, normal and emergency parachute deployment, and the dreaded parachute landing fall, or PLF.

Steve's first jump found him in unfamiliar territory from the beginning. He donned his flight suit and jump boots as always, but to this was added his back-mounted T-10 military round canopy and chest-mounted reserve. Everyone was quiet on the climb to altitude.

As the door opened on the UV18B Twin Otter jump plane four thousand feet above the ground, Steve felt the rush of cold Colorado air fill his lungs. He hardly noticed as he inched closer to the exit, waiting for the command every new jumper almost dreaded, "Stand in the door."

Steve quickly moved to his exit position and now had an unobstructed view out the door. Like the countless first jumpers before him, he felt a rush of emotions. Exhilaration. Anxiety. Fear. Adrenaline. All of these things raced through his mind in a split second. Before he had time to think further, the instructor yelled "go," and Steve instinctively leapt out of the aircraft to begin his ten-second plummet toward the Colorado landscape rushing to meet him from below.

As programmed, Steve reached in and pulled the ripcord to deploy his chute and, after what seemed like a lifetime, his free-fall was stopped with a pop and a jerk signifying successful parachute deployment. He looked up, checked his canopy, and immediately searched for the landing zone.

After realizing he was safely within the landing area, he then for the first time had a moment to look around and actually enjoy the parachute ride that he had trained weeks to make. He floated down to earth and executed a PLF, which surely felt as if it were textbook perfect, but was more likely feet, butt, head.

Regardless, any landing a jumper can walk away from is successful, and this is especially true the first time. Steve would make four more jumps to compete the five necessary to earn his military free-fall wings, and with that, he was off to his third and final airmanship program, T-41.

The T-41 program was both a flight indoctrination and screening program for Air Force pilot training using turbocharged Cessna 172s. T-41 was modeled after Air Force pilot training, and the strict academic standards were complemented by a serious flight line program.

The program was designed to weed out those cadets who could not demonstrate basic hand-eye coordination and the ability to think in the air. It was a challenging but rewarding first step to a career in military aviation, and Steve loved it, maybe even more than boxing.

Boxing Buddies

I first met Steve at the Air Force Academy where we were classmates and members of the boxing team. Boxing was not an intercollegiate sport but rather a loosely organized club. The team was run by Coach Eddie Weichers, a legend in the intercollegiate boxing world who coached the Academy boxing program for thirty-eight years.

As a kid from Long Island, New York, I had no previous exposure to boxing, but the Academy would fix that. Every cadet was introduced to boxing as part of the freshman physical education program. It was also an intramural sport, so each of the forty cadet squadrons had a boxing team, and both Steve and I boxed in intramurals. Boxing appealed to Steve because of its scientific nature and immediate feedback. His goal was not to knock somebody out, but to win by points. My interest was less scientific and more primitive—I liked hitting people, even though we all used padded sixteen-ounce gloves and protective headgear.

The club was made up of hardcore boxing enthusiasts, most of whom had never boxed before coming to the Academy. The highlight of boxing season was the Wing Open Boxing Championships, a tournament culminating under the lights in the Clune Arena in front of a packed house. Steve mentioned boxing often in the letters he wrote home, especially as the Wing Open approached.

I got to know Steve well during boxing because, like me, he was not tall for his weight class, sported a stocky build, and was left-handed. As a result, we trained together often, had a similar fighting style, and because we were left-handed, used different tactics than most of the righties. We also shared a love of music and blasted '70s and '80s rock during our training sessions in the days before exercise headphones.

I got to know him even better during our junior year, as I was able to fight my way to the Wing Open championship bout with Steve as my corner man. I ended up losing a split decision to a senior cadet who went on to win the national championship, but not because of Steve's coaching. He did a great job in my corner and was the only reason my fight was as close as it was.

During our senior year, Steve and I represented the Air Force Academy at the Downtown Athletic Club's "Salute to Boxing Greats" held in New York City in November of 1981, where we both fought our final intercollegiate boxing matches. I will never forget Steve's love and enthusiasm for boxing, as he pushed me to work harder than I ever thought I could. While Steve loved every aspect of boxing, the same could not be said for the rest of his Academy experience.

Rearview Mirror

Like many cadets, Steve had a love/hate relationship with the Academy. Nowhere was that more evident than in the letter he wrote home in mid-February doolie year.

Dear Mom and Dad,

I guess it is that time of the semester again. Only once before have I wanted to quit as bad as now. It's not that I hate this place, it's just I don't think that it is right for me now. I worked so hard during high-school, I didn't enjoy it. I am tired of giving 150% all the time. There are just not enough hours in the day.

Today I was thinking about going home, getting my own apartment, setting up an auto repair shop. I miss the sunshine, working cars, 8 hours of sleep once in a while. Then again I don't want to leave. I am proud of my uniform and of being here.

I'm enjoying my classes. On the other hand there are problems. Face it, I'm different from other people my age. I feel more mature than even the upper classmen. Sometimes I think I take this place too seriously.

While everyone else is bitching about Sami's [Saturday morning inspections], and everything else, I for one say that's a part of being here. You taught me that you must be consistent, and if you let things slide once you are in trouble. Everyone else says things like "I believe in honor in the important things." Too many people are here for a free ride, or just to fly.

You'd be amazed at how few times "service to country" comes to people's lips. People of my generation have no sense of self-sacrifice. I've been through twice as much as most people here and I do the least bitching. If I don't do the job amongst the doolies, it doesn't get done.

I get tired of people who don't realize why they are here. I'm tired of having to be the one to get things done. Nobody else takes things seriously. Maybe my classmates are right, I take this place too seriously. I need advice badly. I don't know anymore. I don't want to kick myself in the ass the rest of my life.

Hopefully things will get better after we get stereos. You both know how important music is to me and to be deprived of it hurts in a way that is very hard to describe. I am not badly depressed, I just don't know what I want to do.

I am a lonely person. Always have been. All I've ever had that I could count on was home. I miss home a lot. I need some help and advice.

Love, Stephen

Steve's family helped him navigate the ups and downs of his four-year Academy experience, and like 841 of his classmates, Steve powered through to graduation on June 2, 1982. That would be the last day Steve and I spent in the same place. Though our Air Force careers would follow similar paths, for the moment we were both more than ready to put the Blue Zoo in the rearview mirror for the last time and venture into the active-duty Air Force. But first, we listened carefully to then–Vice President George H. W. Bush deliver the commencement address, which struck more than a few responsive chords with Steve.

You've been trained and educated by your country to serve your country. That you will serve your country well, I have no doubt. Those who came before you, Academy graduates like Captain Sijan did their duty—in time of war. If you ever are fortunate—if the country is fortunate—none of you will ever be called on to make the kind of sacrifice he did.

You've been taught a lot about the concept of duty while you were here—the idea of service over self, of doing what ought to be done.

You will be entrusted with our nation's most valuable resource, our freedom. Keeping that freedom secure will involve hundreds of kinds of duties...being stationed thousands of lonely miles [away]... flying A-10s. There will be moments when some of you will feel freer than the falcons.

Some of you will come to possess what Tom Wolfe has called the Right Stuff. I can't resist quoting his description of it, that quality which "involved bravery. But...not bravery in the simple sense of being willing to risk your life. The idea seemed to be that any fool could do that, if that was all that was required. Just as any fool could throw away his life in the process. No, the idea here...seemed to be that a man should have the ability to go up in a hurtling piece of machinery and put his hide on the line and then have the moxie, the reflexes, the experience, the coolness, to pull it back to the last yawning moment—and then to go up again the next day, and the next day, and every next day, even if the series should prove infinite—and, ultimately, in its best expression, do so in a cause that means something to thousands, to a people, a nation, to humanity, to God."

Tom Wolfe was writing about the modern, single-combat warriors. About fighter pilots and test pilots and astronauts— about those who found their greatness in the skies and beyond. But they would not have found it, or sought it, even, had they not been doing what ought to have been done. And in seeking their greatness, they were enhancing, and defending, our freedom. Their challenges were our challenges. And their glory became our glory.

In that, perhaps, we realize how much a part of each other we truly are. Once you leave here, where you have spent such an important part of your lives, a great portion of that vigilance will be entrusted into your hands. People you do not know, people you will never see, will be depending on you. And you'll do what there is to be done, and what ought to be done.

For that, we—your country, your parents, your teachers, your president, and I—are very proud of you today. Looking out on all of you, and being here, sensing your happiness in being what you are, I know that in you America has got what it takes—has got the Right Stuff.

Thank you, and God bless.

It would not be the last time the words of Mr. Bush would mean so much to Steve and his family.

PART 3

The Real Air Force

The United States Air Force

Steve was commissioned as a second lieutenant as a proud member of the graduating class of 1982. He was now part of the "real Air Force," which is what he and his classmates called life after graduation, without really being able to describe exactly what that meant. Nevertheless, he was ready to move on. His dream of becoming an Air Force officer came true, making way for his next dream—earning his wings as an Air Force pilot.

UPT

Undergraduate Pilot Training, or UPT, is a fifty-two-week program that molds young Air Force officers into military pilots. UPT takes people who, in many cases, have little to no aviation experience and turns them into jet pilots. The program is intense, unrelenting, and for Steve, a dream come true.

Steve started UPT with class 83-07 on August 23, 1982, at Laughlin Air Force Base in Del Rio, Texas. Located in southwest Texas near the Mexican border, Laughlin's remote location, great weather, and light civilian air traffic made it a perfect UPT base.

The nearby Amistad National Recreation Area provided relief from the Texas heat, but UPT students had little time to enjoy all the lake had to offer. There was a lot to learn in the year at Laughlin.

UPT was divided into three phases, starting with Phase One: academics. The first month was spent almost entirely in the classroom. Steve learned about aircraft systems, local area procedures, safety and life support equipment, weather, navigation, and a host of other military aviation topics. Days spent in the classroom were followed by nights and weekends of seemingly non-stop studying, and Steve loved the challenge. He wrote home about his first experiences in UPT.

September 2, 1982

We've been at it for almost a week and a half. Our days have been averaging 10 hours. The academics is just what we've heard, not difficult, just a lot of information to digest. Our first big test is a week from today on systems. I'm not worried about it. At least we have a 3-day weekend to get ahead.

We are wearing flight suits every day now, which is great. The first few days this week we had various physical activities to break up the day. Today it was a different story. We spent 10 hours in the classroom.

[Earlier this week] we went to life support to learn how to do parachute landing falls. And true to fashion even those who were already jump qualified still had to go through it. True, we got done quickly, but I object to an airman, who has never jumped, critiquing my landings. The landings they were passing were atrocious. I saw several people who are going to get hurt. This training has saved

many people, but it was a waste for 70% of the
class who already had [jump] wings. It broke up
the day though and we made it fun. I am really
motivated and I am looking forward to hitting the
flight line in two weeks.

I can't describe how great the people are. The
treatment we get is phenomenal. I look forward to
going to work. Next week we have a go at the ejection seat simulator and we go through the altitude
chamber so we can experience hypoxia.

Today we practiced the M1 maneuver [a straining
maneuver used to counteract the effects of
gravity, known as G forces] and the Lieutenant
Colonel singled me out (because of my red face) as
doing it well. I am destined for high G fighters.
Unfortunately there is more to flying than that.

After a month of academics, it was time for Phase Two, which
meant heading to the flight line to start flying. Academics would
continue for another nine months, but moving into the flying
phase made sitting in the classroom a lot easier for Steve and his
group of aspiring Air Force pilots.

The Tweet

Moving to the flight line was a step into a whole new world.
Located near the squadron building, the flight line encompassed
acres of concrete ramp packed with over a hundred white aircraft
parked neatly in rows. White lines marked the controlled area
surrounding the aircraft, and spray painted on the ground were
ominous signs reading:

WARNING – Restricted Area
Authorized Personnel Only
Use of Deadly Force Authorized

Entry control points were clearly marked in red and the only way to properly access the flight line. Cross the white lines instead, and you would soon be met by red flashing lights and an eighteen-year-old M16-toting Airman eager to shout the words, "Get down and kiss the pavement!" Between the lines there was a buzz of activity as maintenance troops, brown fuel trucks, and a fleet of blue Air Force vehicles all worked in synchronized chaos to support the hundreds of training sorties flown daily. Add the scream of jet engines and the smell of burning jet fuel known as JP-4, and you can get a sense of why Steve and his fellow students were so excited to begin training on the flight line.

Flying in a military jet trainer was a big change even for seasoned civilian pilots, starting with the uniform. Like his fellow students, Steve wore a fire-resistant flight suit, which was notoriously hot in the summer and cold in the winter. His life support equipment included a parachute to be used in the case of an emergency requiring ejection, plus a flying helmet complete with an oxygen mask which covered his nose and mouth. All of this equipment, coupled with the heat of a Texas flight line, and the ever-present smell of burning jet fuel, was enough to make some sick to their stomachs before they ever strapped in to fly. Steve took the experience in stride and quickly adapted to his new surroundings and helped others do the same.

While UPT was for the most part an individual sport, there were some team dynamics at work. Most of the students in his class had come directly from the Academy, many of whom he already knew. The atmosphere of Steve's pilot training class was one of camaraderie, which was important. A close-knit class could band together to protect a weaker member. The stronger students would help those in trouble, and Steve made a genuine effort to help anyone struggling, even though these same students would be competing down the road for a limited number of coveted fighter assignments. As flying started, Steve and his classmates set aside thoughts of what they might fly later, turning their attention instead to their newfound love.

UPT flying began in a small, stubby-winged side-by-side jet trainer, the T-37 Tweet. The Tweet, also called the six-thousand-pound dog whistle, was best known for its shrill, high-pitched engine noise. Designed in the 1950s, it was somewhat antiquated by the 1980s and featured a cockpit designed by some fiendish engineer who probably never flew a day in his life. There were dials and gauges scattered everywhere, thanks in no small part to the Air Force's need to upgrade the avionics so that the aircraft could be flown well after its design life had been exceeded.

To Steve, the Tweet was beautiful, and it served as his office for the next five months. No finer place to work, he thought. Tweet training began as all aircraft programs do, with a focus on takeoffs and landings, followed by an introduction to navigation and basic aerobatics. The initial portion of the T-37 phase was designed for two things. First, to eliminate those students who were not suitable for jet training. Second, to move the rest of the students to their first solo.

A normal day during the T-37 phase involved two to three hours of academic instruction, either before or after flying. Flying was broken down into three takeoff time blocks. Steve would generally fly once each day, with the instructors flying two to three times each day. Before flying started, the students were subjected to an intense and occasionally humiliating experience known as "stand up," or emergency procedures (EP) training.

Stand up began when an instructor stood and described a potential emergency situation. On the spot, the instructor selected a student who was required to immediately stand and first recite the boldfaced emergency procedures, which were required to be committed to memory in exact detail. If the student successfully recited the boldfaced procedures, they were then given the opportunity to elaborate on the answer. If the student successfully recited the applicable boldfaced and follow up procedures, their reward was no punishment. Steve was called on a dozen times during his UPT experience and was always well-prepared for stand up.

Part of his motivation to study was driven by the fact that any mistake during stand up resulted in the immediate grounding of the student, who was given the remainder of the day to research the error of their way to ensure use of proper procedures next time. Steve did not want EP training to slow his progress, or impact his class standing, so he made sure to be ready every day of UPT. EP training started the process of isolating student pilots and putting them under pressure situations for the purpose of evaluating their ability to perform. Given the fact that these young officers would soon be piloting Air Force jets on their own, this training was critical to their success and ultimately their survival. Indeed, UPT was one long evaluation process.

Steve, like his fellow students, was evaluated and graded after each flight. His academic scores and flight grades were compiled to determine his class ranking, which would impact the type of aircraft the Air Force would allow him to fly upon graduation. In the short term, daily grades were used to assess his performance based on standards known to both Steve and his instructor. Steve established himself early as a gifted young pilot who was motivated both academically and in the air, and he advanced along with most of his classmates to his first jet solo.

First Jet Solo

After months of academics and flying, it was time to fly solo. The day started when Steve and his instructor donned their life support equipment, grabbed their helmets, and made their way to the flight line. Steve completed the preflight, then he and his instructor strapped in, made a normal start, and taxied to the runway. But this ride was different because it involved no area work, only traffic pattern work.

This "pattern-only ride" found Steve's instructor sitting silently as Steve methodically went through all his checklist items and ground operations. They taxied out and, once airborne, made several trips around the pattern, practicing normal approaches and touch-and-gos. After thirty minutes, Steve's instructor told him to land the aircraft, which he did, and taxied back to the ramp. Steve was instructed to shut down the right engine, and his instructor unstrapped, secured the seat, and hopped out of the airplane, giving Steve the thumbs up. Steve then cranked the right engine and went through his normal pre-taxi checklist. He called for taxi and made his way to the runway.

During the taxi out, he glanced over at the empty seat beside him a few times. This was no time to celebrate, but Steve smiled to himself in anticipation of slipping the surly bonds of earth in a United States Air Force jet all by himself. He completed his pre-takeoff checks, closed the canopy, and checked in with the tower for takeoff. Once cleared, he taxied out onto the runway, ran up the engines, released the brakes, and gave it full power. Two hundred pounds lighter thanks to the empty seat beside him, and with half a load of fuel, the Tweet leapt off the runway. Steve was airborne—and alone.

Anticipation gave way to training and self-confidence. Steve was hooked. Everything he had worked for up to this point came together in the cockpit that day. He practiced traffic patterns and enjoyed his trips around the box. In what seemed like only minutes, it was over and time to land. Reluctantly, Steve called for a full-stop landing and taxied back to parking. He secured the aircraft and returned to the squadron, where he was met by both congratulations and tradition. Congratulations in the form of handshakes, and tradition in the form of a dunking in the solo tank.

His friends and fellow students momentarily turned against him as they grabbed for his wrists and ankles. Steve put up a mild resistance, as was expected, but he didn't fight too hard. He was carried down the hallway and outside where, on the count of three, he was tossed into a pool of water. It felt good after his hot work in the sun and served as a baptism to forever link him to those military aviators who had gone before, and to those yet to go in the future.

After the solo, there was the traditional party, featuring a variety of adult liquid refreshments. It was an important day for those attending, because they had passed a hurdle that a few in their class had not. Those who could not successfully solo, or complete any of the assigned academic phases, were "washed out," meaning eliminated from training and sent out into the Air Force to pursue another career field. Washing out was a sobering reminder about the rigors each student pilot faced, but there was nothing remotely sobering about the solo party.

After soloing, Steve focused on the next hurdles, a series of three flying evaluations called check rides. Check rides were administered by pilots outside of the squadron assigned to the standardization and evaluation flight, known as Stan/Eval. The check ride was a pressure-packed flight where every single aspect of the mission was graded. Check ride grades played a large role in evaluating performance and establishing class rank, and Steve earned strong marks on his three T-37 check rides. As Phase Two came to a close, Steve looked forward to flying something much sleeker and faster than the Tweet.

Talon Time

Phase Three introduced Steve to the Northrop T-38 Talon, a supersonic tandem trainer powered by two afterburning engines. Forty-six feet long and only twenty-four feet wide, the Talon looked like a fighter aircraft. Indeed, T-38 instructors considered themselves more fighter pilots than training command instructors, and Steve's move from T-37s to T-38s was like going from a Volkswagen Beetle to a Ferrari.

The biggest challenge for Steve and his fellow students was that everything was now moving faster. Much faster. Where the T-37 flew in the traffic pattern at 150 knots, the T-38 flew at 300 knots. Everything was faster, which required Steve to think further and further ahead of the aircraft. This phenomenon, known as "getting ahead of the jet," was a term used by instructors to describe to their students what they had to do to effectively fly jet airplanes. It was the ability to think ahead of the where the aircraft currently was that distinguished good pilots from excellent pilots. It was not uncommon to hear that when a student was having problems, they would describe themselves as "way behind the airplane." In time, most students would adjust to this increase in speed, but some could not. Steve made the transition to the T-38 quite naturally, and his strong work ethic kept him "ahead of the jet" for most of Phase Three.

Steve quickly soloed the T-38 and moved through the contact phase mastering aircraft handling, aerobatics, and local area navigation. His first check ride, the contact check, was an important milestone. Steve knew his performance would go a long way in determining whether he was Fighter/Attack/Reconnaissance (FAR) qualified or not. FAR qualification during UPT was the first step toward reaching his dream of becoming a fighter pilot, so he doubled down on his work and was rewarded by an excellent check ride grade.

Next up was the instrument check ride. Instrument flying was an entirely different yet important skill set for an Air Force pilot. At night or in bad weather, Steve would need the ability to fly and fight using only the cockpit flight instruments. Besides practicing instrument flying in the simulator, Steve would complete several instrument rides in the aircraft, flying in the back seat of the T-38 under a canvas hood covering his view of the outside world. It was an unnatural feeling, but the strict rule sets and required adherence to written procedures appealed to his scientific nature, and he had no problems passing his instrument check ride.

Steve's final hurdle was the formation check ride. While formation flying had been introduced in the T-37, formation flying was a high-emphasis skill in the Talon. Where the contact check ride separated the pretenders from the contenders, the formation check ride separated wannabe fighter pilots from future fighter pilots. Steve learned that formation flying combined several important flying elements together into a test of both trust and skill.

Formation Flying

The skill was to fly within three feet of another jet going four hundred fifty miles an hour and maintain an exact position in formation. The trust was to do so without looking out the front window to see where you were going. Steve had no problems with the skill part, but the trust part took getting used to. Understanding the dynamics of formation flying explains why.

The basic flight formation is a two-ship element composed of a lead and wingman. The flight lead is in charge of the formation and responsible for navigation, directing both aircraft through the mission elements, and ultimately the safety of the flight and wingman. The wingman's job is to follow the flight lead, maintain proper position, and support the flight lead as needed. In addition to flight responsibilities, each pilot is also responsible for their own aircraft. In short, there is a lot going on during formation flying, from takeoff to landing.

Steve's first T-38 formation ride started with a formation takeoff. His flight lead taxied out onto the runway, and Steve followed, lining up beside and slightly behind his lead, separated by just ten feet of wingtip spacing. Once ready, his lead made a circular motion with his finger, and both pilots ran up their engines. Steve confirmed all systems were ready and gave his lead a head nod. Lead looked forward, tapped his helmet, and as his chin dropped, released brakes and advanced the throttles to max power. Steve followed, keeping his Talon in position as both jets raced down the runway. Approaching take-off speed, Steve mirrored his flight lead as both eased back on the stick to establish the nose at the proper take-off angle, and seconds later, both aircraft were airborne. Lead glanced over to confirm Steve was airborne, then retracted the gear and flaps, which Steve mirrored. Once cleaned up, Steve smoothly slid into fingertip formation with just three feet of wingtip clearance, never once looking at anything other than his flight lead. The trust he placed in his flight lead would extend to the remaining mission elements as well.

Close formation practice continued once Steve's flight entered the training airspace. With more room to maneuver, Steve's flight lead began a series of smooth aerobatic maneuvers while Steve worked to maintain position and his three-foot wingtip clearance. This "warm-up" exercise not only honed Steve's close formation skills but helped build his confidence as an aspiring fighter pilot. Warm-up complete, the flight lead next directed Steve to close trail, a position one aircraft length behind and slightly below the lead aircraft. Once established, the flight lead began a series of more aggressive maneuvers, challenging Steve to maintain his close trail position. Challenge met, the last exercise of the day was Steve's favorite, fighting wing.

The fighting wing position required Steve to keep his Talon in a forty-five degreed cone behind lead with five hundred to fifteen hundred feet spacing. Fighting wing was a pre-cursor to basic fighter maneuvers, which Steve would learn after UPT if selected for a fighter assignment. The flight lead would run through a series of advanced and aggressive maneuvering including loops, barrel rolls, and rapid reversals. Steve's job was to stay in the cone, using three-dimensional maneuvering. Fighting wing required quick thinking, fast reactions, and Steve loved every minute of it. Now low on fuel, the flight began recovery back to Laughlin, but there was one important hurdle left—the formation landing.

If the formation takeoff opened the door to trusting your flight lead, then the formation landing sealed the deal. Picture this— Steve was tasked with landing a jet flying at two hundred miles an hour, ten feet from another jet landing on the same runway, while looking out the side window. Sounds crazy, but that's exactly what he did.

As the flight lined up on final approach to land, Steve was moved out of fingertip formation back to his ten-foot spacing for the formation approach and landing. Lead leveled off at a thousand feet above the ground, slowed the flight to 220 knots, then signaled Steve to lower the gear and flaps. Once configured for landing, Steve gave the "thumbs up" signal and wiggled his fingers and toes in an effort to stay relaxed. Three miles from touchdown, the flight slowed to 170 knots and began down the glideslope. Steve confirmed he was lined up to land on the left side of the 150-foot-wide runway and resumed his focus on lead. He maintained formation position, and nearing the ground, began to notice the airfield coming into view. One quick final check, and he returned focus to his flight lead all the way to touchdown. As soon as his wheels hit, he pulled the engines back to idle, opened the speed brakes, and transitioned his attention to the runway ahead of him to slow his Talon while maintaining position on "his" side of the runway. Landing complete, the flight taxied back to parking and shut down. Mission complete.

After a series of formation rides adding more advanced elements, including four-ship formation work, Steve was ready for his final check ride. As with other check rides, Steve was well-prepared, had a great attitude, and flew a great ride. Nearing the end of UPT, it was time for Steve to fill out his "dream sheet," the Air

Force form on which he expressed his aircraft preferences. The class also compiled a yearbook, and Steve's yearbook entry read as follows:

Steven R. "Haruna Mc-" Phillis

Name:	Steven Phillis
Home Town:	Rock Island, Illinois
College:	Blue Zoo
Spouse:	N/A: but taking applications
Ambition:	To go to test pilot school
Favorite book/movie:	The grade book
Favorite saying:	If you run with the big dogs ...
Favorite drink:	Strohs
Favorite maneuver:	Heimlich
First choice of aircraft:	A-10

Assignment Night and Graduation

Assignment night was held a few weeks before UPT graduation and was an event of great joy or great sorrow, depending upon the young officer's aspirations and performance. At Laughlin Air Force Base, assignment night was a festive event fueled by excitement and adult beverages. Like many of his classmates, Steve desperately wanted to be a fighter pilot and hoped assignment night would propel him into a fighter cockpit. Competition to join the fighter world was keen, with only the top graduates selected for a fighter assignment. Steve was one of the top students in his class, so his dream of flying the A-10 was within reach.

One by one, each student's name was called, and their anticipation was replaced by a photo of the aircraft they were assigned to fly. Steve impatiently waited his turn. After what seemed like an eternity, his name was called; and moments later, up flashed a picture he would never forget—a photo of the Fairchild Republic A-10.

Weeks later, on August 4, 1983, Steve earned his Air Force pilot wings. Graduation from UPT was a family affair, so following an old Del Rio tradition, after Steve was awarded his wings, he removed them from his chest and broke one of the wings off. Handing the wing to his mother, he asked her to keep it in a safe place, but to never let it touch the other half, as letting the wings touch was said to be bad luck. Both Steve and his mother would make sure that they never did, and days later, Steve left Del Rio, Texas for the next stop on the road to becoming a fighter pilot.

LIFT

Alamogordo, New Mexico is home to the White Sands National Monument and Holloman Air Force Base. In the summer of 1984, Steve checked into the 436th Tactical Fighter Training Squadron "Black Aces" at Holloman as a Lead In Fighter Training (LIFT) student. LIFT was the gateway to fighter aviation, where new pilots were given initial indoctrination into basic fighter maneuvers and tactics.

LIFT students flew the AT-38, modified versions of the Air Force's T-38 they all had recently flown in pilot training. The AT-38 was basically a T-38 that has been repainted in blue camouflage and fitted with a rudimentary armament control and heads-up display system. To Steve, it was a most beautiful sight.

The "heads-up display" was nothing more than a combining glass mounted on the dashboard in front of the pilot on which a basic adjustable gun sight was projected. There were no computers added to give the AT-38 any modern avionics capability, but it was wired to carry a gun pod, rockets, or practice bombs on the centerline pylon for air-to-ground training.

LIFT helped new pilots develop into fighter wingmen by teaching the fundamentals of fighter aviation. Advanced formation flying, basic fighter maneuvers, surface attack, and air combat maneuvering are all introduced to ease the transition to the complexities of fighter aviation. LIFT taught Steve about the skills he would need as a fighter pilot, and more importantly, what it meant to be a fighter pilot.

The Fighter Pilot

Steve loved being a fighter pilot and all that came with it. There is no one best way to describe what it means to be a fighter pilot, but "fighter pilot" describes an attitude more than a job. It starts with a burning desire to accomplish the mission. Since the mission of most fighter pilots is to put warheads on foreheads, tactical skill and the ability to make your machine perform is the ultimate measure of success.

Fighter aircraft are complex machines, and missions are demanding and sometimes dangerous. No matter, because while fighter pilots may lack a great many things, confidence is not one of them. Indeed, the best fighter pilots have a quiet yet unyielding confidence in their ability to get the job done, and they look no further than to their fellow fighter pilots for validation. Steve's quiet confidence, born at an early age, allowed him to fit right in.

The only peer to a fighter pilot is another fighter pilot. Nobody else quite measures up. At the end of the day, they only care about what other fighter pilots think of them, and reputation is everything. It doesn't matter where you're from, it doesn't matter who you know, it only matters what you know and what you can make your machine do.

In the end, being a fighter pilot is a blend of confidence, courage, respect, and focus few will ever really understand. It's always about what's right and never about who's right, where rank means little and skill means everything. Blended together with an ultra-high *esprit de corps*, intolerance for naysayers, and modest disdain for anyone who is not a fighter pilot, you can begin to understand exactly what it means to be a fighter pilot.

Steve developed one of his core fighter-pilot skills on the bombing ranges not far from Alamogordo.

Range Rides

Located sixty-five miles north of Holloman were the Red Rio and Oscura bombing ranges, where Steve would get introduced to the world of surface attack. The training syllabus included low- and high-drag dive bombing, strafe, and rocket attacks. The first ride introduced the box pattern, which was essentially a traffic pattern used on the range to space out aircraft for individual bombing passes.

Range rides were normally four-ship flights supervised by instructor pilots in the air and range control officers on the ground to ensure flight safety. Good idea since hurling a perfectly good AT-38 at the ground at 450 miles an hour was not without risk. Pilots learned to monitor and control dive angle, speed, and release points to blend weapons accuracy with survival.

Steve's first range ride introduced him to the "conventional pattern," a rectangular ground track designed to create aircraft separation and sequencing for each bombing pass. His AT-38 was equipped with six BDU-33s, twenty-five-pound practice bombs containing a spotting charge to create a cloud of smoke on impact. He rolled in on his first ten-degree dive-bomb pass, located the center of the bombing circle, and hurled his AT-38 at the ground. His job was to manage airspeed, dive angle, and aim point to arrive at the weapons-release point to drop the BDU-33 into the center of the target, known as the bullseye. Once in position, he pressed the "pickle button" under his right thumb, felt the bomb come off, and started his safe escape maneuver. Climbing away from the ground, he looked out and saw the cloud of white smoke rising just short of his target. He had just dropped his first bomb and was hooked on ground attack.

Steve learned that AT-38 bombing passes were executed at ten- and twenty-degree dive angles. Gun passes were made into the strafing pit, and they were riskier because the goal was to fire at the last minute to concentrate bullets on target while pulling off before flying below the safe altitude or foul line. Each pass was scored for accuracy, with closer always better and direct hits best. Scores were made public, so of course Steve competed for the best scores on every pass for two reasons. First, bragging rights, but second, there was money at stake.

Steve got introduced to Quarters on his first range ride. Quarters was a simple but serious part of any range ride. Every pass was worth a quarter, and every pilot placed a quarter on the table for each pass. The pilot with the best first pass took the first four quarters, and so on until every pass was counted and every quarter was gone. There was nothing quite like the sound of quarters jingling in your flight suit pocket walking out of the debrief—a sound Steve would hear often during his flying career. While Quarters was certainly a part of fighter-pilot culture, it was the debrief itself that really opened up Steve's eyes to the new world he was entering.

Welcome to the Debrief

Mission planning, briefing, and execution during LIFT were joint efforts between the instructor as flight lead and student as wingman. While these were familiar tasks to Steve, the biggest change he noticed at LIFT was the heavy emphasis on debriefing. UPT debriefs were quick and mostly painless, while in LIFT they were anything but.

Debriefs were detailed, intense, and a vitally important part of life as a fighter pilot. Each aspect of the mission was debriefed, from preparation to start, taxi, takeoff, mission effectiveness, and recovery. Every single tactical event was reviewed, dissected, and critiqued in excruciating detail. Training time was limited, and it was crucial to get every ounce of learning out of each sortie.

The key to effective debriefing was to identify the root causes of every success or failure. This required brutally honest exchanges between the pilots. No punches were pulled, excuses were not tolerated, and rank did not matter one bit. In the spirit of improvement with no personal attacks intended, pilots would dig deep to capture best practices and fix errors going forward. Debriefs were where the real learning occurred, and Steve soaked up every drop he could find.

Speaking of soaked up, debriefs often ended up at the bar. Everyone would grab a cold one, move to the squadron bar, and talk about flying. Some would share something they learned, others would tell stories of mistakes they'd made or seen, and others just listened. No matter what your style, some of the most important lessons learned at LIFT were learned in the bar. And where there was a fighter bar, there was usually a crud table nearby.

Crud

Steve got introduced to his first of many fighter pilot traditions at his first Friday night at the Holloman Officers' Club, or O Club. The game was crud, but it was no game. It was a deadly serious competition with a lot at stake. The losers had to buy the winners' drinks.

Crud is a team game played around a large pool table, or more properly, a snooker table. It involves the cue ball as the shooter and a colored object ball. The object of the game was to eliminate everybody on the opposing team. Last-man-standing kind of thing.

The game is normally played between competing fighter squadrons, with each squadron designating an equal number of team members. Each player starts with three lives, and the teams alternate shots. Lives are lost when someone shoots the object ball into one of the pockets or prevents the other team from doing so before the object ball comes to rest.

Like all true competitions, crud features a referee, normally a fighter pilot from a squadron not currently playing. In crud, the referee is God, whose decisions are final, and anyone quibbling with the ref's decision is assessed a life on the spot. The first player eliminated from the game buys the referee a drink since it was important for the ref to maintain the same level of inebriation as the players.

There are a lot more rules to crud, all of which keep the game moving and allow for a lot of strategy around the table. With names like "no six," "double kiss," "balls," "blocking," and "buffoonery," it takes a little time to learn the nuances of winning play. Crud also features varying degrees of physical play.

Basic crud, or crud played before cocktails, was a no-contact event. The shooter had free run of the table, and the next shooter from the opposing team also had free run to position themselves to retrieve the cue ball once played. A slightly more aggressive version allowed for visual blocking, while an even more aggressive version allowed shooters to hold their position after releasing the cue ball. The most aggressive form of crud, and the one that usually broke out after many drinks, was combat crud.

Combat crud was pretty much a full-contact version, meaning shooters and the next opposing player would battle side by side for position at the table. Players could aggressively hold their position and move to impede progress. More than a few ice packs, and an occasional stitch or two, were needed after a long Friday night of combat crud.

The first team to be completely eliminated was deemed the loser, and their punishment was twofold. First, they got kicked off the table and had to wait their turn to play again. Second, they had to buy drinks for the winners. If the winners had a virgin, meaning a player who lost no lives, it meant doubles, but the losing team got to pick the second drink. Ten times out of ten, the second drink would be a shot of Weed.

Weed

Jeremiah Weed, or just Weed, is a one-hundred-proof bourbon-based liqueur that for reasons largely unknown is the shot of choice for Air Force fighter pilots. Weed is definitely an acquired taste. Problem is, no one really ever acquires a taste for it. As a result, it was kept in the freezer and served as an ice-cold shot. Makes the burn and experience a little more bearable, but only a little.

The United States Air Force fighter pilot community likely kept the brand alive based upon how much they consumed over the years. Weed was available in every Air Force fighter pilot bar around the world, and Steve was happy to do his part to keep the tradition alive. He drank many a shot during his time at Holloman while learning to play crud, courtesy of the LIFT instructors and the F-15 pilots stationed at the 49th Tactical Fighter Wing across the ramp.

Steve learned the real truth behind Weed, which is still true today. Weed makes ordinary men do extraordinary things, and extraordinary men do the impossible. A few shots of Weed were all it took to go from zero to hero, or from calm and cool to hair on fire. His crud game and Weed skills would reach new heights at his next assignment: conversion training to his first fighter aircraft.

PART 4

The Mighty Hog

RTU

Davis-Monthan Air Force Base in Tucson, Arizona, known as DM, was the site of A-10 conversion training, known as Replacement Training Unit, or RTU. After completing LIFT, Steve was finally going to get his hands on the A-10, which the Air Force called the Thunderbolt II, but one look at it and you knew in an instant why everyone else called it the Warthog. In late November of 1984, Steve checked into the 358th Tactical Fighter Training Squadron "Lobos" to start a new chapter in his fighter aviation career in the Warthog.

RTU started out with weeks of academics, where Steve learned everything there was to know about the A-10. First up were basic systems, which included fuel, electrical, environmental, hydraulics, engines, avionics, instruments, and flight controls. What jumped off the pages was the fact that the A-10 was designed with survivability in mind. Not a fact that his family needed to know much about, but the old Timex slogan, "It takes a licking and keeps on ticking," was most certainly built into the Warthog's design.

The A-10 sported enhanced survivability features, given its anticipated mission of providing close air support to troops in close contact with the enemy. Titanium armor around the cockpit, redundant fuel and hydraulic systems, and two engines all contributed to aircraft survival. Perhaps the most elegant survival feature was the flight control system, which Steve studied at great length.

The primary flight control system uses pushrods from the stick connected to redundant cables to dual hydraulic actuators connected to the primary flight control surfaces. The actuators are powered by separate hydraulic systems, and the aircraft is fully controllable with a single hydraulic system. If any of the flight control surfaces become jammed, the pilot has emergency disengage switches to free the jam. If all else fails, the Manual Reversion Flight Control System (Manual Reversion) is an emergency system adequate for making moderate maneuvers for a safe return to base and landing.

Manual Reversion is used when dual hydraulic failure is pending or has occurred, and it essentially bypasses the hydraulic system in favor of direct manual flight control surface activation. Steve practiced the use of Manual Reversion in the simulator, and in the aircraft during RTU, so he had both faith and confidence in the Manual Reversion system. After mastering aircraft systems, it was time for more serious matters. After all, the difference between a fighter and unscheduled airliner is weapons, and in that category, the Warthog packed quite a punch.

The Mighty Hog

The A-10 was designed for the close air support mission, so speed was not a requirement. In fact, some thought that a slower airplane with greater loiter time would be an advantage for close air support. If slow is what they had in mind, slow is what they got. Jokes about the A-10's lack of speed were endless, but

Steve didn't care one bit. He knew his Warthog had it where it counted most.

The A-10 could carry sixteen thousand pounds of weapons on eight under-wing and three under- fuselage stations, including nearly every conventional bomb, rocket, and air-to-ground missile in the Air Force inventory. It could carry all that firepower a long way and stay on station for a long time.

Range and on-station time could be extended by aerial refueling, which Steve got to practice for the first time in RTU. The refueling receptacle was located on the nose of the aircraft, directly in front of the pilot, making it easy to see for both day and night refueling operations. But without question, Steve's favorite feature of the A-10 was located just in front of and below the refueling receptacle.

The Gun

What made the A-10 so special in the hearts and minds of hog pilots was the gun. The A-10 was designed and built around the GAU-8 Avenger, a seven-barrel 30mm hydraulically driven Gatling-type gun, which was advertised as a tank killer.

The gun was huge, weighing in at over four thousand pounds fully installed and measuring over nineteen feet long. It was the size of a Volkswagen Beetle. It fired an amazing sixty-five rounds per second at exit velocities in excess of three thousand feet per second. This is especially impressive given each bullet weighed almost a pound.

The A-10 carried almost twelve hundred rounds of ammunition, enough for eighteen seconds of continuous fire, or twelve to fifteen trigger pulls of combat employment. For combat operations, the gun was loaded with both High Explosive Incendiary (HEI) and Armor Piercing Incendiary (API) rounds. HEI rounds contain a mechanical fuse that ignites the explosive mixture inside the bullet upon impact. The API rounds are even more effective, using a depleted uranium projectile against hard and armored targets.

The reaction between high-velocity depleted uranium and steel caused the round to catch fire upon penetration, causing catastrophic damage to any target. Used against a manned target, the results were devastating. In fighter-pilot speak, shooting a tank with the gun resulted in "a mix of hair, teeth, and eyeballs." Sorry, but that's how we talk.

Shooting the GAU-8 Avenger was pretty straightforward. A fixed gun cross was projected on the heads-up display, or HUD, an angled combining glass mounted in front of the pilot on the windscreen. The weapon was boresighted to, or aligned with, the gun cross. Place gun cross on target, squeeze trigger, bullets arrive seconds later. In the hands of a skilled pilot, the 30mm rounds were effective from two miles away but required precise aircraft handling for the accuracy needed in combat.

Turn and Burn

The large wing and control surfaces coupled with a sophisticated flight control system made the A-10 highly maneuverable. RTU was Steve's first real experience with high maneuverability, since the trainers he'd flown were not quite as nimble as the Warthog. Maneuverability was a key component of the A-10s offensive and defensive capabilities, and understanding a little bit about the subject is needed.

When aircraft maneuver, they generate forces with and against gravity called g-forces, or Gs. If the pilot pulls back on the stick to raise the nose against gravity, it creates positive Gs. Positive Gs push the pilot down into the seat and force blood down toward his feet. Left unchecked, positive Gs can result in pilot blackout and loss of consciousness. The A-10 had a maximum design load of just over seven Gs.

Pilots have two tools to counter the effect of positive Gs. First, they wear G-suits, which inflate to restrict the flow of blood to the lower extremities. Second, they execute a straining maneuver to force blood back into their head. Pulling Gs is not comfortable, but fighter pilots are well-trained and get lots of practice, making it second nature. Anyone who has ridden a roller coaster has experienced brief exposure to G forces, so just imagine being at the controls of the world's largest roller coaster as it hurtles through the air.

If instead of pulling back on the stick, the pilot pushes forward, the nose tracks down with gravity creating negative Gs. Negative Gs are extremely uncomfortable since they force blood into the pilot's head, and no G-suit or straining maneuver can prevent this. In addition, negative Gs pull the pilot out of the seat toward the canopy, which is also super uncomfortable. The A-10 had a maximum design load limit of negative three Gs, which is right at the limit of what humans can withstand for any length of time.

Time to Fly

Finally, the day came when Steve would pilot the A-10. What seemed like a dream such a short time ago was about to come true. It was the thrill of his young life, and he was delighted to get back out on the flight line in December of 1984. At that time, the A-10 was one of only two fighter aircraft in the Air Force inventory manufactured in only a single-seat version. As a result, the A-10 was the only fighter, aside from the F-117 Nighthawk stealth fighter, in which a pilot flew his very first sortie alone: a fact frequently mentioned by A-10 pilots.

Steve had been up close to the Warthog before, but walking out for his first sortie, he paused for a moment to notice that the A-10 was one big fighter. Fifty-three feet long with a fifty-seven-and-a-half-foot wingspan made for a lot of airplane, and its dark green camouflaged paint scheme made it look menacing. It was not only big, but tall. Standing under the wingtip, he could not reach up and touch it. After completing the walk around inspection, he climbed the ladder and sat down in the seat, his head fourteen feet off the ground.

Start, pre-flight checks, and taxi went as briefed. As he pulled out onto the runway, he couldn't help but notice how great the visibility was; and before he knew it, he was advancing the throttles to max power for takeoff. Moments later, Steve and his Warthog slowly climbed into the Arizona sky for the beginning of what would become a beautiful friendship. His instructor pilot, flying alongside in his own A-10, watched as Steve navigated to the training area and flew a series of confidence maneuvers to get a feel for his new office. The Warthog was stable, agile, and an absolute dream to fly. Steve was in love.

Area work complete, Steve returned to DM to practice a series of visual approaches before making a full stop landing. He taxied clear of the runway and back to his parking spot, where he shut down and unstrapped. He climbed down the ladder, spoke briefly with his crew chief, and started his walk back to the squadron. After a few steps he stopped, turned around, and smiled at the thought that he was now a lifetime member of an elite fraternity— he was a single-seat fighter pilot.

The Single Seat Fighter Pilot

Being a fighter pilot is one thing. Being a single-seat fighter pilot is altogether something else. After weeks of academics and simulator training, the day finally comes when you get to pilot a fighter aircraft all by yourself. No one looking over your shoulder or second-guessing your decisions. No one there to ask for help. Just you and the machine, and the feeling is incredible.

First up is the feeling of anticipation. After dreaming for decades, training for years, and studying for months, Steve's expectations were through the roof. Next is excitement. Watching fighters fly by at the Academy and A-10s buzz around the skies at DM was the stuff of movies. Finally, it was validation. Years of hard work, dedication, and success added up to a day when the United States Air Force would toss Steve the keys to one of their high-priced toys and let him take it for a spin all by himself.

One of the most appealing aspects to many fighter pilots is the prospect of flying a high-performance combat airplane alone. While there are some missions and aircraft that require a crew of two, fighter pilot purists look at two-seat fighters as aberrations. Any self-respecting fighter pilot would much prefer to fly a single-seat fighter. This leads many to a single-seat fighter pilot mentality.

A single-seat fighter pilot learns early on in his training that success or failure in the air will ultimately be his own responsibility. There is no opportunity to blame someone else for your failure. This environment breeds an attitude of independence like few others. The single-seat fighter pilot learns to rely on his own skills and abilities, and though he is educated as to his own limitations and weaknesses, he rarely admits to either. Additionally, single-seat fighter pilot mentality leads to incredible levels of competition in a profession that can exact the ultimate price for failure. The bottom line is this: the single-seat fighter pilot has the attitude that he and his machine can do any mission assigned, at any time, and under any circumstances.

This undoubtedly sounds like a huge ego trip. It is. So much so, that only a single-seat fighter pilot can check the ego of another; there is no one else who is worthy of the respect and admiration of most fighter pilots. But this makes sense. A single-seat fighter pilot is entrusted with a highly complex machine capable of delivering massive firepower, death, and destruction on a moment's notice. He must master not only all details of his weapon system but is required to have an in-depth knowledge as to the threat and capabilities, weapons, and tactics. On top of this, he will be given a specific set of mission objectives to accomplish a tactical task but given the flexibility to decide how best to achieve this mission.

In sum, young men in their early twenties are given an awesome amount of responsibility and are asked to lay their lives on the line, if necessary, to accomplish this goal. Perhaps the true spirit of the single-seat fighter pilot can be found in this toast, "Here's to us. Damn few like us, and most of them are dead."

Time to Fight

His first few flights were designed to familiarize himself with takeoffs, landings, and basic aircraft handling qualities. As advertised, the Warthog was nimble and simple to fly, and Steve took to it quickly. After mastering the basics, it was time to move on to more serious matters.

While Steve found flying the A-10 easy, fighting with it was an entirely different matter. At times, he would have to fly the Warthog right up to its performance limits with aggressive control inputs. Other times demanded extreme precision and almost imperceptible control inputs. Most of his attention was focused outside the jet to keep a close eye on where he was going, but he still needed to keep track of the hundreds of switches, dials, lights, and displays inside. A solid grounding in the fundamentals was absolutely required for success.

First up was basic fighter maneuvers, or BFM. Steve got introduced to BFM in LIFT, but applying what he learned in the highly maneuverable A-10 was something altogether different. BFM pushed Steve to maximum perform the jet with aggressive horizontal and vertical moves. He learned the "break turn," a high-G defensive turn used to defeat threat aircraft and missiles, and to prevail in three-dimensional fights using extreme nose-high and -low turns. It was a roller coaster of stop-to-stop stick inputs, and he loved every second of it.

On the other side of the flying spectrum he learned aerial refueling, a skill requiring small and precise throttle and stick movements. Refueling started by intercepting the tanker, no small feat in a fighter with no radar. After the rejoin, he was taught to slide his Warthog directly behind and below the converted Boeing 707 airliner into a precise window so that the tanker boom operator could plug the metal refueling pipe into the Warthog's nose. Once contact was made and fuel started flowing, Steve would be required to hold the jet still during this aerial dance four miles up until the refueling offload was complete, and he was trained for both day and night refueling.

The balance of RTU flying was spent on surface attack rides. The flight would depart DM on a low-level navigation route to the Gila Bend range complex. There, Steve would learn a wide array of attack profiles, include thirty-degree dive, twenty-degree low-angle low-drag, fifteen-degree pops, and level deliveries. Each delivery helped prepare him to bring the fight to the enemy.

Air combat in the Warthog was not just about offensive, as any self-respecting enemy would try to fight back. It was important to Steve, and his family, that he learn how to live to fight another day, so he took great care to study the defensive capabilities of the A-10 as a way to round out his RTU experience.

Defend Yourself!

"Defense in depth" is a great description of the A-10's survivability features, starting with its basic design. The cockpit featured armor plating able to stop small- and some medium-caliber bullets. Two separate and redundant electrical and hydraulic systems power major components, and two cooler-running turbofan engines were separated in reinforced pods mounted above the fuselage. Taken together, they help the Warthog survive hostile fire. After design follows detection.

The Radar Warning Receiver (RWR) detects the presence of radar emissions and provides visual and aural warnings of threat radar systems. A round scope mounted at the top of the instrument panel just left of center provided type, bearing, and rough range to the threat. Audio signal heard in the headset was generated to alert the pilot to any new threat. Once detected, it was time for countermeasures.

The A-10 was equipped with electronic and expendable countermeasures in the form of the ALQ-131 electronic countermeasures (ECM) jamming pod, chaff, and flares. Steve was exposed to these capabilities in RTU but would learn a lot more about them in the years to come. For now, he knew enough to graduate from RTU and head to his first operational fighter assignment.

PART 5

Alex

Alex

Steve had finally arrived. The long car ride south brought him to the gates of England Air Force Base in Alexandria, Louisiana-Alex for short. Steve rolled down his window as he approached the main gate in the spring of 1984 and was hit in the face by a blast of hot, humid, Louisiana air—something that would take some time to get used to. Flashing his ID card to the gate guard, he was admitted.

Steve was headed to the 75th Tactical Fighter Squadron "Tiger Sharks," his first fighter squadron, a unit that holds a special place in every fighter pilot's heart. Your first fighter squadron is a lot like your first girlfriend. You're not sure what to expect, and you sure don't know everything you need to, but you know that you are glad to be there. Unlike a first love, however, the feeling is not mutual.

The fighter squadron draws its strength from experience. Since new pilots lack experience, they sap the operational squadron by diverting training resources. Although this cycle is a necessary part of building and maintaining a combat-ready air force, a new pilot is still a drain.

The benefits of having young lieutenant fighter pilots are the influx of new ideas and their almost unbridled energy and enthusiasm. This spirit and energy helps the unit maintain the intensity necessary for the high state of readiness required of front-line combat units. As a result, the new lieutenants are welcome with more or less open arms into the world's most elite fraternity.

Getting to a front-line unit is every young pilot's dream, and now Steve's dream was coming true. He had passed all the hurdles so far and now commanded a certain level of respect. The first part of his long journey was almost over, but he was now faced with the task of upgrading his status to a mission-ready pilot, which would involve several months of training in the mission qualification training (MQT) program. Steve's arrival at Alex also immediately qualified him to join a unique group within the squadron: the LPA.

LPA

Every squadron had a chapter of the LPA, or Lieutenant Protection Association. Eligibility for membership was simple—be a fighter pilot with the rank of lieutenant. Nothing more. The LPA looked after its own and helped pass down information to new arrivals: who were the best pilots in the squadron, how to get more flying time, and how to best handle the mundane additional duties normally delegated to lieutenants. While not a complete "us-against-them" group, the LPA was an organized and recognized part of the squadron that could be counted on to keep the bar stocked, always be ready to fly, and be available for a party at a moment's notice. Steve loved being part of the LPA.

Because experience counts for so much in the fighter business, Steve's most important goal was to get on the flying schedule as much as possible. Flying hours were everything. They were required for upgrade to flight lead, mission commander, and instructor, but more importantly were required to become a better fighter pilot.

In a group where performance meant everything, no one wanted to be the worst pilot in the squadron. If you asked, you would not find a worst pilot in the squadron. But as the least experienced, the LPA feared that one amongst them might be in that category, and they did everything they could to gain experience, improve their skills, and demonstrate their talent to others.

What's in a Name?

Steve proved his talent early with a strong showing in the MQT program. He quickly learned the local area procedures, was always well-prepared to fly, and had a great attitude. As he neared the completion of MQT, he got closer to another fighter pilot milestone: a call sign.

Fighter pilots get call signs, not nicknames. Your pet has a nickname. Your friend has a nickname. Fighter pilots get call signs, and Steve knew that the fighter pilot world could be brutal. Nowhere was this more evident than during the assignment of call signs.

There were a few unwritten rules about call signs. First, you don't get to pick your own call sign, ever. It is given to you by a group of your peers, typically in some mild to moderate state of inebriation. Second, if you hate your call sign never show it. The more you hate it, the more it's yours for life. Finally, your call sign will probably come from some act of buffoonery on the ground or in the air, or be a play off your name.

When Steve completed MQT, the pilots gathered in the squadron bar on Friday night for the naming ceremony. Several options were discussed, debated, and proposed, all with varying degrees of enthusiasm. In the end, the squadron commander, Lieutenant Colonel Bob "Bullet" Coleman, made the final call. Bullet was a Vietnam vet with almost a thousand combat hours and the perfect man for the job. With the last name Phillis, Bullet saw only one choice, and Syph it was.

From that day forward, and for the rest of his flying career, he would forever be known as Syph Phillis. It would be a little bit challenging to explain to his father the medical doctor and mother the nurse, but at the end of the day he was sure they would understand and knew any objection was pointless. Syph embraced his call sign like he did everything else in the fighter business and got back to work.

LSO

The life support officer, or LSO, was typically an LPA job. Steve volunteered for and was selected as LSO soon after MQT. He was sent on temporary duty travel (TDY) to Randolph Air Force Base just outside San Antonio, Texas to complete the two-week Aircrew Life Support Officer Course in the fall of 1984. Returning to Alex, he dove into his duties as LSO.

The LSO was responsible for giving pilots ground training on their survival equipment, which many pilots did not take seriously enough. Steve became an expert on the A-10's ejection seat, survival kit, emergency radios, bailout procedures, and chemical warfare gear. He studied hard and was eager to share what he knew.

LSO was a unique position in the squadron, because Steve got to work with the enlisted life support team. Sure, every pilot interacted with the enlisted maintenance force as part of their flying duties, but for many the interaction ended there. LSO provided Steve a great opportunity to get a perspective from someone other than a pilot, and he learned a lot about the Air Force from his life support troops.

His non-flying duties as LSO complimented his flying duties as a mission-ready A-10 wingman. Getting on the flying schedule was priority number one. Being well-prepared for every flight was number two. Demonstrating his flying skills was a close number three, and one of the ways he could demonstrate his ability was the squadron Top Gun program.

The Top Gun Program

Every operational Air Force fighter unit in the 1980s, including the Sharks, had some form of Top Gun program. Long before the original movie came out in 1986, fighter pilots were engaged in regular training competitions designed to measure those flying skills most relevant to combat capability, namely weapons employment.

Air-to-air units focused on simulated missile and aerial gun employment. Air-to-ground units, like the Sharks, used bombing and strafing ground targets as their measuring stick. The Top Gun program had to be designed as a fair and objective measure of the pilot's weapons-employment skills, so great care was taken to craft a program to meet these requirements.

Each bombing and strafing event completed in training was scored for weapons accuracy using a point system. Scores were added up to determine who the best pilot was for that month, quarter, or year. The Top Gun program extended between the squadrons and generated fierce base-wide competition.

In a peacetime Air Force, full of hyper-competitive fighter pilots, winning was everything. Awards were given monthly in the squadron, and a big presentation was made quarterly in front of the entire wing at the O Club. Every pilot worth his salt wanted to win the competition. While it would take Steve some time to navigate his way to the apex of the Top Gun program, he was getting great realistic training, both at Alex and when deployed to large-scale flying exercises out west.

Red Flag

Steve was chosen as part of a select group of Sharks to participate in Red Flag, the Air Force's preeminent advanced aerial combat training program. Red Flag is a multi-national, large-scale exercise conducted on a huge range complex in Nevada. Hosted at

Nellis Air Force Base outside of Las Vegas, Red Flag's goal was to give pilots their first ten "combat missions" before they ever saw combat. Vietnam taught the Air Force that pilots were most vulnerable to combat loss during their first ten missions. If a pilot survived his first ten missions, he had a much better chance of completing a combat tour relatively unscathed. While the pilots didn't really think of Red Flag as their first combat missions, the intensity and realism of the training was invaluable.

Red Flag missions routinely included over one hundred aircraft, and many joked that during Red Flag, Nellis boasted an air force larger than many countries. The great part about Red Flag, aside from the fact that it was held in Las Vegas, was the opportunity to learn about the capabilities and limitations of all the tactical air forces' assets. It was the first time Steve got to fly with so many different aircraft, and he took every opportunity to meet and share stories with his fellow military aviators.

In addition, these assets were integrated into large scenarios on a fully instrumented range, which tracked the exact position of each aircraft and relayed it to a playback station in real time. This way, if Steve was not flying, he could sit in a large theater and watch the morning's war unfold. It was an incredible learning experience. Steve loved the flying and the after-hours learning at the Nellis Officers' Club bar. It was there that he met, for the first time, an aggressor pilot.

The enemy at Red Flag was simulated by an aggressor force of aircraft flown by specially trained U.S. pilots simulating the tactics of potential enemies, primarily the Soviet Union. Aggressor pilots, known as "Gomers," were not only well-versed in threat tactics but eager to share what they knew with young fighter pilots like Steve. Between the classified briefings in the Red Flag building and the unclassified work at the bar, Steve learned more in two weeks at Red Flag than in two months at Alex. This was true not only for the air-to-air threats, but for the surface-to-air threats as well.

The Aggressors also operated an array of simulated surface-to-air missile sites, which, using radar and optics, would detect, target, track, and simulate engagement of friendly forces. These threat sites were equipped with powerful cameras and video equipment. It was Steve's goal to avoid being captured on film, since video of successful engagements was played during the mass debriefings in front of every pilot at Red Flag, as if the thought of being shot down by a surface-to-air missile wasn't enough incentive to defend oneself.

The A-10s were usually tasked with destroying a valuable ground target. During mission planning, Steve spent a lot of time discussing the threat array and the target-area tactics, both critical to mission accomplishment. The goal was to get in, drop on time, on target, and get out with everybody. Not an easy task given the fact that the hogs had to fight their way in and out.

It was the closest thing the Air Force had to combat, and it undoubtedly saved countless Desert Storm pilots. After the war, many commented that Red Flag was more difficult than combat. While not true for all, it was a testament to the value of the training. Red Flag also gave Steve and his fellow pilots the chance to work closely with the "eye in the sky," an aircraft known as AWACS.

AWACS

The Air Force's Airborne Warning and Control System, or AWACS, is a modified Boeing 707 fitted with a large rotating disc housing a sophisticated radar system. AWACS is able to detect, identify, and track hundreds of airborne targets. Without a radar, the A-10s would usually welcome the opportunity to receive AWACS information about airborne and surface threats.

AWACS could also relay any real-time intelligence information and other directives from the chain of command. The downside was that you had to talk to somebody sitting in an airplane who wasn't a pilot and, although trained, occasionally monopolized the radio frequency, which frustrated more than a few hog drivers. All in all, the benefits outweighed the irritation, and besides, the AWACS controllers could be trained.

AWACS's primary wartime missions including assisting with tanker rendezvous and de-confliction, threat warning, along with command and control. A secondary, but no less important mission, was initial coordination of combat search and rescue, known as CSAR. Red Flag exercises included a CSAR mission where a young LSO like Steve would get dropped off by a helicopter somewhere within the six-thousand-square-mile Nellis Range Complex, after which AWACS would coordinate a CSAR mission ending with a successful pilot extraction via rescue helicopter from a simulated "enemy" territory.

CSAR training was a reminder of the serious nature of military flying. The stakes were high in both peacetime and combat, and Steve's realistic training at Red Flag and back at Alex did not come without cost.

Corky

Steve did not stay connected with many of his Academy classmates after graduation, but he did keep in touch with Donn McCorkindale. "Corky" was an Air Force brat who claimed Texas as his home. He and Steve were Academy squadron mates and friends in Cadet Squadron twenty-eight, the Blackbirds, better known as the Mellow Magpies. Corky's yearbook entry fit him to a tee.

```
He is well known for his plethora of idiosyn-
crasies, such as studying only in bed, eating
peanut butter potato chip cheese sandwiches, and
```

```
wearing clothes that dated back to the Vietnam
era. Nonetheless, as squadron commander, he led
his squadron to become one of the best in group,
showing his ability to lead others.
```

Steve agreed that Corky demonstrated strong leadership skills, which was one of the reasons the two kept in touch.

Corky did well in pilot training and was fighter qualified. He was selected to the fly the Cessna O-2A Skymaster, a Vietnam-era propeller-driven aircraft used to locate enemy positions and call in airstrikes as part of the forward air control mission. The aircraft flew low and slow and placed a lot of demands on a young pilot. Corky was an excellent pilot, but on May 14, 1985, he died piloting his O-2A on a night training mission near Alex. The exact cause of the crash was never determined, but bad weather was a factor in the mishap.

Steve took Corky's loss particularly hard. When a fellow lieutenant, pilot, and Academy classmate dies in an Air Force plane crash, it hits really close to home. Shared memories are still fresh, and it is hard to come to grips with such a young life lost. The fact that Corky died near Steve's home base magnified the tragedy. It was a feeling of loss Steve would carry with him, but he knew he needed to move on. Flying was a dangerous business, and Steve rededicated himself to becoming the best Air Force pilot he could. Corky would have wanted nothing less for his friend.

A Star is Born

Back at Alex, Steve's hard work as LSO, and skills as a mission ready A-10 wingman, got noticed. He absolutely loved flying the A-10 and put in the long hours needed to get better. He was a sponge, soaking up every bit of knowledge he could find, and his thirst was unquenchable. Less than eighteen months after completing MQT, he had upgraded to flight lead, and his face was on the cover of the base newspaper dated Friday, November 8, 1985.

75th TFS Pilot Earns Top Award

The 75th tactical fighter squadron recently selected First Lieutenant Steven R. Phillis as its top pilot of the quarter for the period July 1 through September 30. Lt. Phillis earned the award based on a measurement of his pilot skills, weapons delivery scores, and academic testing, according to Lt. Roger R. Radcliff, 75th TFS Commander.

"Lt. Phillis has done an outstanding job, both as an A-10 pilot and as a squadron life support officer." Col. Radcliff said. "He has made outstanding contributions to the squadron and to the 23rd tactical fighter wing."

"Selection as a top pilot in a fighter squadron is an honor," Col. James L. Jamerson, 23rd TFW Commander, said. "The competition is tough — no pilot would have it any other way! Lt. Phillis earned it."

Lt. Phillis is the wing project officer for the Air Force academy squadron program. He was an active participant in the reserve officer training corps and cadet visitation program last summer. He is also an A-10 flight lead.

"The 75th TFS is a team," Lt. Phillis said. "No one excels without the support of the squadron. My success is the unit's success, and the squadron has my thanks for their support."

Steve got some justifiable ribbing from the LPA, but his success at Alex continued and resulted in the dream of every first-assignment stateside fighter pilot: a second operational fighter assignment to an overseas location.

PART 6

Suwon

Suwon

Suwon Air Base in the Republic of Korea was a twenty minute flight from the North Korean border, and it was a great place to be a fighter pilot in the 1980s. Steve arrived at Suwon in July of 1986. At that time, the Reagan administration was aggressively pursuing its anti-Communist agenda, and tensions worldwide were high. Never was this more true than in Korea.

The Korean Armistice Agreement signed in 1953 was not technically a peace treaty, so peace was maintained through constant vigilance in a wartime atmosphere. Suwon Air Base was operated by the Republic of Korea Air Force (ROKAF). The ROKAF took the job of defending their country seriously, which heightened tensions further and kept everybody on their toes. Steve's assignment to Suwon was simply the closest thing to a combat environment an Air Force fighter pilot could find anywhere in the world.

Steve joined the 25th Tactical Fighter Squadron "Assam Draggins," an A-10 squadron detached from its home wing at Osan Air Base. The isolation of Suwon further added to the go to war atmosphere. Without the distractions associated with the wing, the Draggins focused entirely on the task at hand—maintaining the peace and preparing for war. It was a job and environment that Steve relished.

Steve arrived in Suwon as an experienced flight lead and was quickly checked out in the local area. His intensity and experience soon earned him a job as the chief scheduler for the squadron, one of the most important and influential positions that a young captain could have, because every pilot really cared about only one thing—flying.

Steve's experience also helped him successfully compete for selection as a combat search and rescue (CSAR) pilot. He was given extensive training in procedures surrounding the downing, protection, and recovery of a pilot lost to enemy fire. Because the Suwon A-10s were expected to halt North Korean armored thrusts down several anticipated attack routes across the border, the A-10s would be flying in an environment rich in both targets and threats. Because of Suwon's mission, the Draggins considered themselves as the first and last line of defense from a North Korean invasion.

With this responsibility came the duty to take risks in a combat situation which would likely result in the loss of some aircraft. No one wanted to think about getting shot down, but everyone wanted the best pilots available for CSAR duty should they suddenly be forced from the relative comfort of their cockpit to parachute ride down into the middle of a North Korean attack.

The Draggins were also unique in the A-10 community because repelling an invasion would center on medium- and high-altitude tactics. The sheer number of guns in a large invasion made low-altitude flying near-certain death. As a result, the Draggins routinely practiced medium- and high-altitude bombing and strafe to ensure they were ready if called.

Steve was completely immersed in the mission. To leave no doubt, he decided to print business cards, which looked like this:

Steve "Syph" Phillis
Casual Hero

Wars fought for a reasonable rate
Parties attended, no extra cost.

When only the best will do,
dial 243.0 and ask for 30MM.

While most of the card is self-explanatory, the last line needs clarification. "Dialing 243.0" means selecting the military air distress frequency monitored by all military agencies worldwide, while "asking for 30mm" refers to the A-10's 30mm gun and the firepower it delivers. In sum, it means "call me on the radio and I'll be right over to blow something up for you with my gun."

Suwon's go to war atmosphere was also fueled by the living conditions. Every pilot lived in a Korean War–era two-story Quonset hut. Everything was covered with layers of barbed wire. Since Suwon was a remote tour, even married pilots were stationed there for one year unaccompanied. This meant that the pilots were around each other around the clock. When a unit is immersed in a daily go to war attitude, men bond together like in few other circumstances. The Quonset huts at Suwon had a room for each pilot, the doors for which were never locked.

Steve's room was noteworthy for the amount of hi-fi stereo equipment and electronic gear that he had amassed. His entertainment center was complimented by hundreds of videotapes, including the fighter pilot classics *Caddyshack*, *Animal House*, and *Stripes* to name a few. Steve's room was often the scene of a Sunday afternoon movie accompanied by a shared Scotch. He found a new friend to drink with, along with a new roommate, when Lieutenant Greg Henderson checked in to Suwon.

Hendo

"Hendo" Henderson arrived at Suwon as a first-assignment lieutenant with the right attitude as far as Steve was concerned. Steve loved to teach and looked for new wingmen who he could mold into warriors. Hendo fit the bill to a tee.

Hendo arrived at Suwon straight out of RTU, and Steve took him under his wing and brought him into the scheduling shop. Scheduling in Korea was organized much differently than in the States, with the chain of command flowing from squadron commander and the operations officer directly to the scheduler. This fact gave the schedulers tremendous power in the squadron. Steve and Hendo used it to shape the Draggins into a lethal fighting force, but the workload meant that everyone worked long, hard hours, and no one more so than Steve.

Steve and Hendo got along so well they became roommates upstairs in what they called the "wild side." It just so happened that the people more inclined to get fired up and rowdy lived on the second floor. They referred to the first floor as the "brownie floor," because as Friday night rolled around, the guys living on the ground floor would sit around cooking brownies while the upstairs gang hit the town hard. But before hitting the town, they absolutely had to make an appearance at the club.

The Samurai Scarf

Suwon, like most Air Force installations, boasted the weekly Friday-night bonding ritual that began after work when all the fighter pilots piled into the All Ranks Club. The pilots quickly adjourned to the comfort of the pilot bar where they knocked back beers and shots of Weed as a warm-up. Of course, what warm-up would be complete without a few games of crud?

Steve loved to play crud. He was agile, tenacious, and absolutely hated to lose. Everyone knew in an instant the games were getting serious when he pulled out his white samurai scarf and tied it around his head, which he seemed to do every Friday night. The origins of the scarf are not completely clear, but Steve was a huge fan of the Teenage Mutant Ninja Turtles. Steve raced around the crud table, made more than his fair share of shots, and drank his fair share of shots as well.

Steve was not afraid to mix it up around the crud table and was often the first one to initiate more contact with the opposing team. The night always ended up with a full-blown combat crud game, with the crud table often ending upon its side, and broken glass littering the crud room where shot glasses had been smashed to the toast of "Fuck Communism!" Before leaving, Steve would lead the group in song.

The Songmeister

Scotch, Weed, and for that matter any alcohol brought out Steve's singing talents. Indeed, he fancied himself as quite the song-meister and would often lead the group though a set of fighter pilot classics near the end of the Friday evening's on-base events. He would stand on the broken glass, drink in hand, and get every-one's attention by singing out a very loud, "me, me, meeeeee." Then it was time to sing.

To be clear, fighter pilot songs are not like other songs. For starters, most cannot be sung in the presence of children. Second, they are typically passed down pilot to pilot at the bar while drinking. Third, they must be sung at full volume regardless of who else is present. With names like "Swing Low," "Sammy Small," and "The Balls of O'Leary," each was special in its own way, and all had an aviation twist of some kind. Steve's all-time favorites included "Dear Mom," "There Are No Fighter Pilots Down in Hell," and "Throw a Nickel on the Grass."

Dear Mom

Dear Mom, your son is dead, he bought the farm today
He crashed his OV-10 on Ho Chi Min's highway
It was a rocket pass and then he busted his ass
Mmm, mmm, mmm
He went across the fence to see what he could see
And there it was as plain as it could be
It was a truck on the road with a big heavy load
Mmm, mmm, mmm
He got right on the horn and gave the DASC a call
"Send me air, I've got a truck that's stalled"
The DASC said, "That's all right, I'll send you Draggin Flight"
FOR I AM THE POWER!
Those fighters checked right in, gunfighters two by two
Low on gas and tanker overdue
They asked the FAC to mark just where that truck was parked
Mmm, mmm, mmm
The FAC he rolled right in with his smoke to mark
Exactly where that fucking truck was parked
And the rest is in doubt 'cause he never pulled out
Mmm, mmm, mmm
(With Reverence)
Dear Mom, your son is dead. He bought the farm today.
He crashed his OV-10 on Ho Chi Min's highway.
It was a rocket pass and then he busted his ass.
Him, Him, Fuck Him!

There Are No Fighter Pilots Down in Hell

Chorus (Repeat after each verse)

Sing Glorious, victorious
One keg of beer for the four of us
Singing Glory Be to God that there are no more of us
'Cause one of us could drink it all alone.
Damn near...Pass the beer...To the rear...Of the squadron!
Oh, there are no fighter pilots down in hell,
Oh, there are no fighter pilots down in hell,
Oh, the place is full of fear, navigators, bombardiers,
But there are no fighter pilots down in hell,
Oh, the bomber pilot's life is but a farce,
Oh, the bomber pilot's life is but a farce,
With the autopilot on, reading comics in the john,
Oh, the bomber pilot's life is but a farce,
Oh, there are no fighter pilots up at wing,
Oh, there are no fighter pilots up at wing,
The place is full of brass, sitting round on their fat ass,
Oh, there are no fighter pilots up at wing,
You can tell a navigator by his ass
You can tell a navigator by his ass
Oh, it's forty inches wide, getting wider every ride,
You can tell a navigator by his ass
Oh, there ain't no fighter pilots down below
Oh, there ain't no fighter pilots down below
They're all way up above, drinking whisky, making love
Oh, there ain't no fighter pilots down below

At the end of the night, before things really got out of hand, there was often this tribute.

Throw a Nickel on the Grass

Oh, Halleluiah, Halleluiah
Throw a nickel on the grass—Save a fighter pilot's ass
Oh, Halleluiah, Oh, Halleluiah
Throw a nickel on the grass and you'll be saved

If you can imagine a dozen or so drunk fighter pilots singing in full throat, with gusto, and mostly off key, then you get the idea. After Friday night warm-ups were complete, the gang would return to their rooms to shower and change for a Ville run.

Ville Runs

The Big Ville, or just Ville, was an area of bars located outside the gates of Osan Air Base, while the Skoshi-Ville were the bars outside of Suwon. Most Friday nights found the pilots racing off from Suwon to the Ville in Osan. Their warm-up activities usually meant that few were fit to drive, though they always did.

Steve, never one to be left out, was an active participant. He felt strongly that the squadron should work hard together and play hard together. He genuinely liked people and wanted everyone to have a good time, meaning he often ended up as social director for the evening. This Friday night ritual fell squarely within Steve's comfort zone.

Steve could not fairly be characterized as the guy who always lit his hair on fire or got himself out of control. He would have one or two less drinks and would always take responsibility to make sure that no one got way out of hand, or way too drunk to drive. Of course, after drinking, who is to say where that line is, but if there were anyone present who would know best where that line was, it would be Steve.

The Ville run started with the whole group of pilots traveling to a few favorite locations to enjoy the beverages of their choice. Most of the pilots, including Steve, drank the local beer. Korean beer is not like American beer and is certainly not like European beer. Without getting too much into the details, the fact that the Koreans used formaldehyde as the preservative in their beer should say it all. Often pilots joked that drinking Korean beer would prolong their life by starting to preserve their brain cells early. In fact, all they were doing were pickling the ones they killed each Friday, but they never gave that more than a passing thought.

After drinking their fill, it was time to drive home, but of course this was no big deal to a group of invincible and now-bullet-proof fighter pilots whose job would be to singlehandedly defeat what was anticipated to be the largest invasion since World War II if the North Korean Army came south. The car ride home was made even sportier by the pilots' antics. Racing across the dark Korean countryside, they used beer cans as "chaff and flares." The idea was to throw beer cans at the cars behind you, which the driver was required to avoid. This was, of course, made easier since everyone was wearing a new pair of cheap sunglasses, which never made it through the night. And such was a typical Friday night in Suwon, Korea.

The Next Step

Steve's talents as social director were surpassed only by his talents as an A-10 pilot. He upgraded from flight lead to mission commander, then to instructor pilot, but he set his sights even higher. In the fall of 1987, Steve reached one thousand hours of A-10 flight time, an important milestone. Important because it was an unwritten requirement to attend the Air Force's premier fighter pilot training program—Fighter Weapons School.

Formally called the Fighter Weapons Instructor Course, or FWIC, "Weapons School" boasted the most competitive selection process in the Air Force. Dozens of highly qualified A-10 pilots from units around the world competed for a handful of slots in each class, and as good a pilot as Steve was, there was no guarantee he would get selected.

With strong support from the leadership at Suwon, Steve submitted in his first FWIC package and was not selected. The news hit him hard, and for the first time in his flying career he had doubts about his future. He took stock of his experience, picked himself up, and applied for the second time, hell bent on getting selected for Weapons School. Just a few months later, he would get the nod and quickly packed his bags for Las Vegas.

FWIC

Steve returned to Nellis Air Force Base, the location of his Red Flag experience years ago, just after New Year's Day in 1988. Aside from Red Flag, Nellis hosted the USAF Tactical Fighter Weapons Center, and as home of the Weapons School, was considered "Mecca" by most fighter pilots. Steve was fired up to attend the A-10 FWIC, the feature-length version of the Navy's abbreviated Top Gun program. Weapons School was nothing like the Hollywood version, except perhaps for the great flying.

Weapons School arose out of the Air Force's need for highly skilled fighter pilots and instructors. The Weapon School's goal is not just to make each fighter pilot the "ace of the base," but to mold them into the premier instructor in their squadron. The peacetime fighter force is constantly in a state of training, so the demand for FWIC graduates is endless.

Steve would be schooled in every facet of A-10 employment, from basic tactics all the way to advanced multi-force composite operations and everything in between. It would be his job to make sure his squadron is ready to go to war. Indeed, the weapons officer was the tactical heart and soul of the squadron charged with delivering maximum combat effectiveness, and few commanders would dispute this fact.

Weapons School was a grind. Steve completed over 250 hours of academics, platform instruction training, and regular written exams. The flying was world class, but each sortie was a ten-to-twelve-hour affair if everything went right, and he flew over thirty sorties during the five-month program.

The hallmark of FWIC flying was the debrief, which normally lasted four to six hours, some longer. No stone was left unturned, from mission planning and preparation, to briefing, ground ops, departure, recovery, and tactical execution. Each engagement was reconstructed on a chalkboard, and every line had to be just right. A thorough analysis of what went right, what went wrong, and how to improve next time was completed for each engagement.

Even for an experienced fighter pilot, Weapons School was daunting. There was an aura and mystique about the program and instructors reinforced daily by the school's go to war mentality. If Steve felt intimidated, it never showed. He was methodical, thorough, and cool as a cucumber under the heavy pressure of FWIC debriefs.

So strong was Steve's performance that during graduation in late April he was named a distinguished graduate and awarded Outstanding Graduate for best overall achievement based upon leadership and instructor potential. In a private ceremony fueled, of course, by alcohol, the FWIC instructors presented each new graduate with their coveted "Target Arm," the patch worn by weapons officers.

After the ceremony and a good night's sleep, Steve awoke to the sight of his flight suit hanging in the closet. Though his vision was a bit blurry, he could clearly see the left shoulder now adorned with his Target Arm. It looked good and it felt good, and even a dull headache could not diminish the pride he felt in joining the long line of weapons officers who preceded him. He felt the obligation to earn the patch every day, and he returned to Suwon with new knowledge and a renewed commitment to making the Draggins the best fighter squadron on the planet.

Back at Suwon

Steve returned to Suwon to complete the last six months of his two-year assignment, energized by Weapons School and armed with new ideas. He studied the North Korean army and their tactics and, along with his fellow pilots, concluded that the Draggins needed to evolve their training. If the North Koreans came south, the sheer number of anti-aircraft guns they would bring would make low altitude A-10 employment a suicide mission. The answer—more medium- and high-altitude training.

In the late 1980s, Korea-based A-10s were some of the few in the world practicing medium- and high-altitude attacks, and Steve made a compelling case they needed even more practice. The idea was that weapons delivery from higher altitudes would keep the Warthogs out of range of most of the guns, making them more survivable. Steve's plan was met with some resistance, but he persisted and eventually convinced most everyone that he was right. Like it or not, Draggin pilots regularly practiced bombing and strafing from all altitudes.

Nearing the end of his tour in Korea, Steve felt good about his contributions to the combat capability of the Draggins. Since this was the only meaningful measure of success to Steve, it was all he needed. His stellar work at Weapons School, coupled with his success at Suwon, earned him an assignment most would covet—a trip to the beach.

PART 7

The Beach

Welcome to the Beach

Myrtle Beach, South Carolina is a vacation resort along the Atlantic coast renowned for pristine beaches, golf courses, and a host of great bars and restaurants. In the late 1980s, it was home to Myrtle Beach Air Force Base, headquarters of the 354th Tactical Fighter Wing. The Wing's activities centered around three Warthog squadrons with twenty-four jets each. As a stateside fighter wing, the 354th's mission was to prepare for deployment to any hotspot in the world on short notice. The challenge at "the Beach" was that with enemies thousands of miles away, and all that sunshine, it was difficult to maintain a "go to war tonight" attitude.

Make no mistake; the Beach was a great place to be stationed as an A-10 pilot. But with no real prospect of war to be found, and the Air Force now more than fifteen years removed from combat flying in Vietnam, the Beach was a resort town that happened to have an A-10 wing nearby. Enter Captain Steve Phillis.

In November of 1988, Steve drove through the front gate of the Beach on his third operational A-10 assignment, fresh off his two-year remote tour at Suwon. With a noticeably short haircut and dip of Copenhagen, he stood out immediately. His first order of business was to check into his new unit, the 353rd Tactical Fighter Squadron, known as the Panthers. Steve quickly assessed the state of his new squadron and concluded in short order that the Panthers needed his help and experience.

Deploying a fighter squadron overseas involved an enormous amount of logistics and maintenance support. This meant that the 354th Wing could only deploy one squadron at a time, so leadership had to devise some way of racking and stacking the three squadrons. Using unit performance metrics and a wing-wide Top Gun competition, the squadrons were designated Alpha, Bravo, and Charlie. The Alpha squadron was considered the number one unit and would be the first to deploy, usually followed by the Bravo squadron. The Charlie squadron was typically relegated to remain at home station and considered a source of additional airframes and pilots if needed. Steve learned the Panthers were firmly entrenched as the Charlie squadron and immediately set out to change that.

Steve could not get over the vast differences between the Beach and Korea. Contrary to the Beach, Suwon featured round-the-clock vigilance, a heightened state of alert, and complete focus on combat capability. Truth be told, he was not sure the Beach was the right place for him. If Korea was the closest thing to a combat zone Steve had ever experienced, then Myrtle Beach was the closest thing to Hollywood that you could find in the A-10 world. Ready or not, as a highly trained pilot with overseas experience, he would soon turn his attention to the Panther pilots.

Back to Stateside Flying

The Beach was a single-wing base, meaning everything on the base was centered on the flying operations. Without the distractions that come with additional missions and supervision, the

Beach, like Suwon, fostered a cohesive spirit among the pilots. On the downside, the lack of "go to war" urgency was replaced by the emphasis on neat uniforms, shiny boots, and Top Gun competitions. It was an adjustment that Steve found difficult to make, and one he resisted, but he had a job to do.

Moving the Panthers up from Charlie squadron required a team effort, so Steve's first task was to draw together several pilots who were stationed with him in Korea, as each shared his passion for tactical excellence and mission focus. The "Korean Mafia" was criticized at first, because all they would talk about was how great it was in Korea. But as time went on, their spirit and enthusiasm began to draw the squadron together as a fighting unit. Much to Steve's delight, Hendo joined the Panthers following his tour at Suwon and added another strong voice in support of tactical excellence.

Steve pushed the Korean Mafia hard because he wanted their enthusiasm to rub off, yet at first resisted shifting the Panthers' focus from tactical employment to the Top Gun program. As Panther weapons officer, the only thing that mattered to Steve was the squadron's warfighting prowess. Everything else was rubbish. However, he would have to adjust to the realities of a stateside fighter assignment.

As the tactical epicenter of the Panthers, Steve needed the blessing of squadron leadership for his training plan. Lieutenant Colonel Charlie Thrash commanded the Panthers, and his extensive experience at the Beach included duties as squadron pilot, instructor pilot, mission commander, flight commander, and operations officer before assuming command of the 353rd. Charlie knew what it took to succeed at the Beach and had definite opinions about what needed to be done.

One afternoon, Steve was called into Colonel Thrash's office to discuss the direction in which his squadron was going. Steve stuck to his deeply held belief that tactical employment must come first. Charlie, understanding Steve's point, knew that in order to build that tactical skill, he had to raise the level of flight performance in the squadron; and to do that, they needed to win Top Gun.

Steve thought for a moment about the dilemma before him, but before too long, his military training and instincts kicked in. He was immediately keen on the idea and let his commander know in no uncertain terms that the squadron's weapons program would focus first on winning the wing Top Gun competition. He marched back to the Panthers' weapons shop and announced their new focus, never for a moment letting his personal feelings show through. Steve's next step was to get to know the key players at the Beach, so he started at the top and worked his way down.

Who's Who in the Zoo?

The Myrtle Beach wing commander was Colonel Sandy Sharpe, the consummate fighter pilot who was respected, admired, and even liked by almost everyone—a rare quality for a fighter wing commander. The respect came from his flying ability and his two combat tours as an F-4 pilot in Vietnam. After two postwar tours in the F-4, he moved to Nellis in 1980 to help start the F-117 stealth squadron and became that squadron's first operational commander.

Sandy Sharpe was well liked because he was a people-oriented commander who tried to fit the needs of his people as best he could within their operational commitment. His personal involvement and tireless work demonstrated the "leadership by example" skills most admired by fighter pilots, and Steve liked him immediately.

Next Steve met again with Colonel Thrash and the rest of the Panthers' leadership. All were friendly, yet each sized up their new weapons officer while he did the same. He needed to sort out the herbivores from carnivores and knew it wouldn't take long once he started flying. Finally, he started meeting the pilots. He took time to meet with each one separately, to introduce himself and start laying the groundwork for his weapons program. After a quick local area check out, he dove into his duties as weapons officer and also took time to check out the Beach's off-duty opportunities.

The Beach Party

Much to Steve's delight, the social scene at Myrtle Beach included Friday night at the O Club. It was a regular event not to be missed. Like Suwon, the O Club was a gathering place for pilots from every squadron and included several hours of rowdy drinking and games. Although quiet by nature, Steve could be the life of the party—just add alcohol.

Steve did not confine his O Club activities to just playing and drinking. He could often be found in the main bar area, talking tactics or discussing any subject with anybody. His slow, deliberate way was a quality that pulled people in. While he was comfortable talking about most anything, he was especially at home with anything related to flying. Steve was just as comfortable sitting with a Scotch and talking one-on-one with a colonel as with a lieutenant. It was just who he was.

The Beach was likely going to be a three-year assignment for Steve, so he decided to buy a house. All who visited thought it a nice house, fully equipped with massive amounts of stereo and TV gear he bought in Korea. Once he got settled, he started entertaining, and his house was often the site of squadron parties. Steve loved to entertain and mingle with everyone to make sure they had everything that they needed. He was the consummate host and wanted everyone to feel comfortable when they came into his home. Not one to let go of tradition, he would sometimes emerge from his room wearing his Korean party suit, which was essentially a onepiece polyester leisure suit embroidered with logos from each squadron he had served in. Steve loved to wear his party suit, even if he was grossly out of style.

Parties at Steve's house included Panther pilots, wives, and girlfriends. In time, as people got to know Steve better, others joined in. Hendo was a regular at Steve's parties and introduced him to a group of girls who had befriended the Panther bachelors. This group of fired up and outgoing people formed the core of Steve's social scene at Myrtle Beach. Often they would pick up the phone and call one of the pilots and say, "we are having a party over at your house tomorrow night." In response, the pilot would say, "sure thing," and the gang would then assemble for an evening of partying. This group gave new meaning to the "work hard, play hard" way of life, and it suited Steve just fine. Such was the life of a fighter pilot.

The Patch

Steve had definite ideas about how his fighter squadron should work. Yes, *his* fighter squadron. The commander was the boss, but as weapons officer, also called the "Patch," the Panthers' performance would be more of a reflection on him than anyone else. Armed with ideas from Alex, Suwon, and most importantly Nellis, he got to work on his program.

When it came to fighter flying, Steve was old school, which meant he placed great emphasis on flight discipline. One day, Steve was leading a four-ship range ride when on the way home an overzealous wingman chimed in on the radio to announce he had listened to the Myrtle Beach Air Terminal Information Service (ATIS) recording and had information for the flight. This was heresy to Steve.

Every flight member was required to monitor frequencies assigned by the flight lead, and absolutely nobody else, which meant the wingman had left frequency to check ATIS without permission. Rather than wait for the debrief, Steve slowly and methodically went through each of the four frequencies the flight was monitoring, asking where he heard the ATIS, to make the point that his wingman was not authorized to leave the frequency without permission, and that his misconduct would not be tolerated. Flight discipline was a skill Steve constantly demanded and one that would pay dividends in the squadron Top Gun program but, more importantly, in the future should combat operations arise.

Each stateside fighter base had a "checkered flag" location, a country or area of potential trouble that the unit was preselected to support should hostilities start. The idea was as part of peacetime training, the unit would become familiar with the terrain, military forces, and general political situations that existed, so that if trouble erupted the unit could be quickly deployed to that area of the world and have some expertise upon arrival.

The Panthers' checkered flag location was Iran, and Steve made it a point that the Panthers would know everything about Iran and the surrounding area in the Arabian Gulf. Helping him every step of the way were his friends in the Korean Mafia. While every member played an important role in shaping the Panthers, Steve had a special place in his heart for his Suwon roommate Hendo.

Sharon

Hendo easily plugged into the Beach social scene when he arrived, and as one of the Panther bachelors, he befriended most of the girls in no small part because of this looks. He formed an especially close relationship with a woman named Sharon. Not romantic, but close friends.

Sharon Taflen was an executive secretary and aerobics instructor in her late twenties who was part of the single Panthers bunch. She first met Steve at a party and didn't notice him at first, but they had something in common. Sharon, like Steve, wanted to make sure that everybody was taken care of. She was the one who would go out to the store to get more food or beer when necessary. Often while out on the town, she would end up being the designated driver. It was in the role of co-hostess that she first noticed Steve. Steve noticed Sharon too.

Barely topping five feet, Sharon was a fireball. Energetic, enthusiastic, talkative, and cute. She was a no-nonsense girl who told it exactly as she saw it, while at the same time being a true people person. Her work as an aerobics instructor kept her petite figure slim and fit, a quality not lost on Steve. Sharon was born in West Virginia and lived there until age twenty-two, when she moved to Myrtle Beach. While fully involved in Myrtle Beach's fast-paced social scene, she had not met an Air Force pilot during her first five-plus years at the Beach.

One summer day in 1989, a girlfriend called up and said that she had met an Air Force pilot and wanted Sharon to go with her to Myrtle Beach's Officers' Club. Sharon didn't know the Officers' Club from a golf club, but she reluctantly agreed to accompany her friend. There she met, for the first time, a fighter pilot. Interesting, she thought.

They were a group of guys who obviously shared her passion for partying, and their togetherness and clean-cut appearance were appealing. She met several of the guys but quickly established a friendship with Hendo. They shared similar outlooks on life and were often seen talking together at parties. Hendo thought Steve needed to meet Sharon, and vice versa.

Steve noticed Sharon before she noticed him. One time at a party, she was talking to a group of friends when Steve came up from behind her and rested his arm around her neck. He looked at her and said, "You know, I've been thinking that I ought to ask you out on a date. Do you think you might go?"

She said, "Well, I don't know. Probably."

And then he said, "Okay. I just wanted to know,"—and he walked off. It would be weeks before he would ask again.

Steve had decided that he wanted to ask Sharon out. Hendo approached her on the subject, and she was not interested. But Hendo was relentless in his opinion that she should go out with him. She relented but told Hendo, "If he tries to kiss me, I am out of here." Steve made the call and Sharon accepted. The day of their first date she talked to a girlfriend about what they might do that evening. The girlfriend offered only one piece of advice. Do not go see the movie *When Harry Met Sally*.

Steve picked Sharon up, and the first topic of conversation was what to do. Steve's answer was, "I thought we would go to the movies and see *When Harry Met Sally*." Uh-oh, she thought. They went to the movie, and both survived the ordeal. Leaving the movie, the question then came up, "Well, what would you like to do?"

Sharon said, "I would like to grab a six-pack of beer and go for a walk on the beach." Her wish was his command. They walked the beach that night admiring the stars.

Steve began pointing out the constellations. He didn't know just one or two. He seemed to know them all. She thought it was great that he could name them, and she was captivated by his knowledge. The walk on the beach over, they went back to Steve's house, sat down, and talked about movies.

Much to her surprise, she learned that one of Steve's favorites was *The Sound of Music*. It was one of her favorites too, so they sat down and watched *The Sound of Music* together. After the movie, they just sat and talked and talked and talked. Before either one knew it, it was four in the morning. It was too late to go home, so Steve asked Sharon to sleep in his bed while he slept on the living-room couch. She would have no part of that, and insisted she wanted to sleep on the couch. He refused, and she refused to give in. The result? Sharon asked Steve to take her home, and he obliged.

Their first date was over. Sharon, now back at her apartment, thought back to a moment during *The Sound of Music* when Steve put his arm around her. It felt good, it felt right, and it was so comfortable. Sharon was amazed how they were both so relaxed and just enjoyed each other. As she drifted off to sleep, she knew she had found the one for her.

A Second Date, and Beyond

Steve called the next day to tell Sharon he had a really good time. Three days later, he called again, and when she picked up the phone heard, *"It's the Great Pumpkin, Charlie Brown,* would you like to come over? I'll make you dinner." She accepted on the spot, as she was not the type of person who needed a lot of time to make a decision.

Sharon arrived at Steve's house, which she had seen before as a party guest. While he was making dinner, Sharon got a closer look at his house and discovered Max, a large dark brown teddy bear wearing a Hawaiian shirt. She thought it was funny for a fighter pilot to have a big teddy bear, and interesting that they shared a common interest in *The Great Pumpkin*. After dinner and Peanuts, of course it was again time for *The Sound of Music*.

After the movies, they again sat and talked about anything and everything. Steve loved any conversation, and Sharon loved to talk. Since they were both a little older than the company each kept, they shared similar views on many subjects. Family, religion, current events, and the people at the Beach were all regular topics of conversation. After another long evening, Steve walked Sharon to her car and opened the door. While it was hard to say who exactly who made the first move, together they leaned in for their first kiss.

As summer turned to fall, Steve and Sharon spent more and more time together. They watched football, went out on the town, and were seen together at most Panther events. In early

November, Steve again invited Sharon over, and during dinner said, "I know I just met you, but I am going on a ski trip in February, and I want you to think about it. You don't have to answer me now, but I would like you to go."

Immediately Sharon thought, *It is November, and he is thinking about February. Obviously he thinks he is going to keep me around for a while.* She turned to Steve and said, "I'll go."

He said, "You will? You thought about it?"

She said, "Yes, I thought about it, and I will go." Steve was thrilled, and at this point was spending more time out with Sharon than anywhere else, except work.

From Charlie to Alpha

Back at the office, Steve put in long hours and a lot of work as the Panthers' weapons officer. While it goes with the territory, Steve embraced the challenge of steadily improving both the Panthers' combat skills and Top Gun scores. Along the way, Lieutenant Colonel Rick Shatzel was named as the new squadron commander, and he strongly supported Steve's march toward improvement.

As the months went by, the Panthers moved up from Charlie to Bravo, then from Bravo to Alpha. Steve was pleased that the Panthers would now be the first ones out the door if anything popped up in the world, even if there was no sign of that happening anytime soon. His hard work was recognized when he was selected the Panthers' Junior Officer of the Year for 1989. The citation read in part:

```
Congratulations on being selected as the 353rd
Tactical Fighter Squadron Junior Officer of the
Year for 1989. You are being recognized for your
outstanding work as the Panther weapons officer.

As the weapons and tactical instructor, your
comprehensive and thorough briefings are superb;
so is your fine attention to detail when it comes
```

with squadron pilots completing all weapons training. Your performance as project officer for back-to-back deployments deserves special mention. The training received was a direct result of superior planning and leadership.

These and many other accomplishments make you particularly deserving of this award. You can take great personal pride and satisfaction knowing that this award represents the squadron's appreciation for your dedication and contribution to excellence. It is your kind of outstanding performance that makes the "Panthers" the best fighter squadron in the Air Force. I am pleased to have an individual of your caliber in the squadron.

Steve was pleased but not overly impressed. He was happy that the two most important things in his life were going well—his job as an A-10 fighter pilot and his relationship with Sharon, or so he thought.

Another Detour

Christmas of 1989 was a joyous occasion for the newly minted Junior Officer of the Year and his girlfriend. Together they celebrated Steve's success, watched all the Christmas movies, and were nearly inseparable. New Year's Eve was even more fun as a couple, and before they knew it, they were off on the ski trip. Everything about the trip was great, and Sharon had a fantastic time. Still, something did not seem quite right to her.

By April, Sharon started thinking, *He is too nice a guy, why is he hanging around me? Any day now I am going to find something wrong with this guy.* And so out of the blue, Sharon called Steve and told him "I don't want to see you anymore."

He asked "Why?"

She said, "I don't know. I just don't think it is going to work." Steve was dumbfounded.

Five days later, Sharon called her best girlfriend, who told her Steve had been calling every day trying to find out what was going on. She asked Sharon, "What happened?"

In response, Sharon said, "I don't know."

She replied, "Well, I just sent Steve to your house."

Sharon said, "You didn't!"

"Yeah, I did."

Steve showed up at the front door and at first didn't say a word. Sharon motioned him in, and once they got back together again, they would never look back.

Sweetness

Second Lieutenant Rob Sweet checked into the Panthers in May of 1990. Rob was fired up about his assignment because he was an east-coast kind of guy, so his A-10 assignment to Myrtle Beach was his number one choice for aircraft and destination anywhere in the world. Rob grew up in Parkersburg, West Virginia and was a 1988 Air Force Academy grad whose cadet squadron was sponsored by an A-10 squadron at Myrtle Beach. Karma.

Rob was relieved to be treated more like "one of the guys" because now he was a qualified A-10 pilot. As an MQT student, his basic military and tactical flying skills were no longer in question, and it felt good to be someplace where he was expected to succeed and rapidly progress to mission-ready wingman status. Rob was a quiet guy, eager to learn but seldom the first one to talk. He fit right into the prevailing view that "lieutenants should be seen but rarely heard."

As the weapons officer, Steve did not get directly involved with Sweet's MQT training, except early on. Before starting to fly at the Beach, Rob reported to Steve for a quick meeting. "Have a seat," said Steve, and Rob obliged. After a very brief exchange of pleasantries, Steve read through Rob's RTU grade book while Rob sat in silence. After a few minutes, Steve looked up and said,

"I'm placing you on special monitoring status for ten-degree dive bombing based upon your performance at DM." Rob nodded, then Steve handed back his grade book and went back to work. Meeting over.

Sweet's introduction to Steve left him with the impression that Steve was a very serious guy, with not much of a sense of humor, and not a lot of extra time for new lieutenants. In sum, Rob was a little scared of his first weapons officer. Rob thought that Steve was a hard-ass—the kind of guy that young pilots would characterize "from the old school," meaning that Steve would expect a wingman to shut up, hang on, and do his job. For the most part, Rob was a good judge of character.

Rob wasted no time getting to work and completed the MQT program in mid-July of 1990. He showed good flying skills, took instruction well, and had no problems with ten-degree dive-bombing patterns. As a mission-ready first-assignment wingman it was now time for a call sign, and after a brief deliberation, "Sweetness" it was. Now that Sweetness was mission ready, Steve got more involved in his training as the two starting flying together.

Off duty, Steve and Sharon's relationship continued to grow. They hosted many a party at Steve's house and spoke or saw each other daily. They kept up their movie-watching habits, and of course, their late-night conversations, but the topics they talked about were getting more and more serious as the months passed.

Return to Rock Island

By the summer of 1990, Steve and Sharon had been dating for nearly nine months, and Steve started talking about getting married. Sharon knew that Steve's Air Force career would include frequent moves, and she told him it didn't matter where they lived as long as they were together. She also knew she was not cut out to handle any of the politics in the Air Force or take any grief from some colonel's wife just because her husband outranked Steve. Rank meant nothing to Sharon, and Steve knew and understood this. He simply expected Sharon just to be Sharon. It was all he needed.

In July, Steve said to Sharon, "I want you to come out and meet my parents." They had originally planned to go in August, but Steve said he couldn't wait, so off they went. Bud and Diane Phillis still lived in Rock Island, Illinois, part of the Quad Cities metropolitan area where Steve grew up. Steve was happy to be home as family was always important to him, evidenced in part by the sheer number of letters he wrote home dating back to his days at the Academy.

Sharon was understandably nervous about the trip. She loved Steve and still knew he was the one for her. She also knew that getting along with his family was hugely important if they were to have a future together. Her fears melted away as the entire Phillis family welcomed her with open arms, and all had a great time during the visit. As wonderful as the visit was, one night Sharon had a wild dream that she found confusing and a bit disturbing, and this is how she told the story years later.

> When visiting the Phillis house Steve slept downstairs on a make-shift bed, and I slept upstairs across the hall from his parents. I was lying in bed and heard stairs creaking and thought, "He is not coming up here with his parents across the hall, I know him better than that." I then heard the door creak and watched it open.
>
> Steve walked into the room and said, "I have to go but I'll be back."
>
> I replied, "Where are you going?"
>
> He said, "Don't worry about it, I gotta go."
>
> I asked again, "Where are you going?"
>
> He said, "Sharon, I gotta go. That is all I can tell you, I gotta go."
>
> Then Steve's face turned to his brother Tom's face, and Tom said, "It's going to be okay."

I asked, "What are you talking about?"
And then Steve's sister Kathy was sitting on her bed saying,
"It's all right. It is going to be okay."

She awoke to an empty room and sat up in bed wondering, "What is going on?" She turned on the light and looked down at the end of the bed and asked again, "What is going on?" She left Rock Island without telling anyone the story, and along with Steve headed back to the Beach to enjoy the rest of the summer.

Invasion

Less than a month later, some guy few had ever heard of invaded a tiny country even fewer knew about and changed the course of history. Saddam Hussein's elite Republican Guards rolled into oil-rich Kuwait and took over the country in a day. That same day, the United Nations Security Council adopted Resolution 660, condemning the invasion and demanding Iraq withdraw immediately and unconditionally. While most Air Force units knew little about Iraq, the Panthers had been studying the area for years.

Iraq invaded Kuwait with the fifth largest army in the world at the time, numbering some one million men. The Iraqis had nearly ten years of recent combat experience against Iran and used equipment supplied primarily by Russia and China. Many experts in the media painted a picture of a modern, well-equipped, and experienced force. On paper, the Iraqis looked like a formidable threat, and their rapid conquest of Kuwait supported that assessment.

The invasion caught the world by surprise, and before long, Iraq was circulating newly printed maps relabeling Kuwait as Iraq's nineteenth province. Saddam believed that the world would hardly notice, and that the United States had neither the interest nor will to do anything about it.

On August 8, President Bush addressed the nation as the entire world looked on. Here are selected portions of his address.

In the life of a nation, we're called upon to define who we are and what we believe. Sometimes these choices are not easy. But today as president, I ask for your support in a decision I've made to stand up for what's right and condemn what's wrong, all in the cause of peace.

At my direction, elements of the 82nd Airborne Division as well as key units of the United States Air Force are arriving today to take up defensive positions in Saudi Arabia. I took this action to assist the Saudi Arabian government in the defense of its home-land. No one commits America's armed forces to a dangerous mission lightly, but after perhaps unparalleled international consultation and exhausting every alternative, it became neces-sary to take this action. Let me tell you why.

Less than a week ago, in the early morning hours of August 2, Iraqi armed forces, without provocation or warning, invaded a peaceful Kuwait. Facing negligible resistance from its much smaller neighbor, Iraq's tanks stormed in blitzkrieg fashion through Kuwait in a few short hours. With more than a hundred thousand troops, along with tanks, artillery, and surface-to-sur-face missiles, Iraq now occupies Kuwait. This aggression came just hours after Saddam Hussein specifically assured numerous countries in the area that there would be no invasion. There is no justification whatsoever for this outrageous and brutal act of aggression.

A puppet regime imposed from the outside is unacceptable. The acquisition of territory by force is unacceptable. No one, friend or foe, should doubt our desire for peace; and no one should underestimate our determination to confront aggression.

Four simple principles guide our policy. First, we seek the immediate, unconditional, and complete withdrawal of all Iraqi forces from Kuwait. Second, Kuwait's legitimate government must be restored to replace the puppet regime. And third, my administration, as has been the case with every president from President Roosevelt to President Reagan, is committed to the security and stability of the Persian Gulf. And fourth, I am determined to protect the lives of American citizens abroad.

Immediately after the Iraqi invasion, I ordered an embargo of all trade with Iraq and, together with many other nations, announced sanctions that both freeze all Iraqi assets in this country and protected Kuwait's assets. The stakes are high. Iraq is already a rich and powerful country that possesses the world's second largest reserves of oil and over a million men under arms. It's the fourth largest military in the world. Our country now imports nearly half the oil it consumes and could face a major threat to its economic independence. Much of the world is even more dependent upon imported oil and is even more vulnerable to Iraqi threats.

We succeeded in the struggle for freedom in Europe because we and our allies remain stalwart. Keeping the peace in the Middle East will require no less. We're beginning a new era. This new era can be full of promise, an age of freedom, a time of peace for all peoples. But if history teaches us anything, it is that we must resist aggression, or it will destroy our freedoms. Appeasement does not work.

As was the case in the 1930s, we see in Saddam Hussein an aggressive dictator threatening his neighbors. Only fourteen days ago, Saddam Hussein promised his friends he would not invade Kuwait. And four days ago, he promised the world he would withdraw. And twice we have seen what his promises mean: His promises mean nothing.

This is not an American problem or a European problem or a Middle East problem: It is the world's problem. And that's why, soon after the Iraqi invasion, the United Nations Security

Council, without dissent, condemned Iraq, calling for the immediate and unconditional withdrawal of its troops from Kuwait. The Arab world, through both the Arab League and the Gulf Cooperation Council, courageously announced its opposition to Iraqi aggression. Japan, the United Kingdom, and France, and other governments around the world have imposed severe sanctions. The Soviet Union and China ended all arms sales to Iraq.

I pledge here today that the United States will do its part to see that these sanctions are effective and to induce Iraq to withdraw without delay from Kuwait.

But we must recognize that Iraq may not stop using force to advance its ambitions. Iraq has massed an enormous war machine on the Saudi border capable of initiating hostilities with little or no additional preparation. Given the Iraqi government's history of aggression against its own citizens as well as its neighbors, to assume Iraq will not attack again would be unwise and unrealistic.

And therefore, after consulting with King Fahd, I sent Secretary of Defense Dick Cheney to discuss cooperative measures we could take. Following those meetings, the Saudi government requested our help, and I responded to that request by ordering U.S. air and ground forces to deploy to the Kingdom of Saudi Arabia.

I want to be clear about what we are doing and why. America does not seek conflict, nor do we seek to chart the destiny of other nations. But America will stand by her friends. The mission of our troops is wholly defensive. Hopefully, they will not be needed long. They will not initiate hostilities, but they will defend themselves, the Kingdom of Saudi Arabia, and other friends in the Persian Gulf.

Standing up for our principles will not come easy. It may take time and possibly cost a great deal. But we are asking no more of anyone than of the brave young men and women of our Armed Forces and their families. And I ask that in the churches around the country prayers be said for those who are committed to protect and defend America's interests.

Standing up for our principle is an American tradition. As it has so many times before, it may take time and tremendous effort, but most of all, it will take unity of purpose. As I've witnessed throughout my life in both war and peace, America has never wavered when her purpose is driven by principle. And in this August day, at home and abroad, I know she will do no less.

Thank you, and God bless the United States of America.

United States military leaders scrambled to assess the situation and dust off old plans. The Pentagon became a swirl of activity, and teams were immediately mobilized into action. The first order of business was to immediately prepare air, sea, and ground forces for deployment.

Mobilization

Soon after Saddam Hussein's armies crossed into Kuwait, Myrtle Beach was put on alert. The Panthers, now Myrtle Beach's Alpha Squadron, were ordered to prepare their Warthogs for deployment. Their deployment destination was unknown, and the pilots were initially told they would probably deploy to Spain to sit and await further instructions.

Every Panther pilot was called in the main briefing room for a classified briefing on the situation. As the pilots were leaving after the brief, squadron commander Rick Shatzel looked right at Rob Sweet and said, "You are not going." As the newest mission-ready pilot in the squadron, Sweet was, of course, disappointed, but not surprised. So in the true spirit of a lieutenant fighter pilot, Sweet replied, "Hey, why don't you leave some of the administrative troops home. I will go over there to do their typing—or anything else that it takes to get over to the desert." He left without an answer but was hell bent on not being left behind.

Generating aircraft for deployment was a maintenance- and logistics-driven exercise that didn't require immediate action by the pilots. The pilots faced a more mundane task—preparing their personal lives and affairs for deployment to an unknown location for an unknown duration. Wills, powers-of-attorney, bank accounts, and all the details that would be critical to families had to be accomplished in a few short days. As a result, while maintenance prepared the A-10s, and the pilots flew a few sorties to confirm operation of the newly installed external fuel tanks, everybody else scrambled to pack their bags and straighten out their personal affairs.

At this point, there was absolutely no thought about how the Panthers would fight the Iraqis. Most of the tactical preparations involved frequent intelligence briefings concerning Saddam, the Republican Guards, and the ground order of battle (GOB) in the Iraqi and Kuwaiti desert.

Steve was not concerned about generating the airplanes. He was in a rush to get his personal affairs in order because he had been selected as part of the ADVON team. This small group of people from the wing would be sent immediately to Saudi Arabia to survey the situation and prepare for the A-10s' arrival. Steve had a lot to do, and Sharon, as always, immediately pitched in to help.

The Question

Two weeks before Steve left for Saudi Arabia, he took time out from his fourteen-hour workdays to spend an evening with Sharon. Steve said, "Let's take a walk on the beach." They walked and talked about the stars like they often did, as Steve seemed to know every star and constellation. After a while, they sat down, and he said, "I need to ask you something."

He said, "You know things are going on right now, I don't know what is going to happen. I just want you to know how I feel about you before anything should happen."

Sharon said, "I know you love me, Steve."

He said, "I want you to know." He stood up, then got down on one knee, pulled out the ring he'd been carrying around for three months, and asked Sharon to marry him.

Of course it was dark, and she was trying to look at the ring but couldn't see it. She yelled, "Yes!" They both cried, then got back in the car, went home, and called both sets of parents.

Based upon current events, Sharon agreed to move into Steve's house. Once settled in, Steve sat down with Sharon and explained that he would be leaving shortly. Being Steve, he was not going to tell Sharon anything about the upcoming deployment and potential tasking because those were his orders, and he followed those orders to the letter.

In the days just before his departure, he sat around the house with a blank expression, wearing a pair of shorts and his boots, waiting for the call that it was time to go. It was melodramatic. Sharon couldn't get him to smile. She was doing laundry and helping him pack his favorite things. She even put on *The Sound of Music* and started acting out some of the parts, dancing around the house. Nothing worked. The only thing Steve did on a regular basis was play Springsteen's "Born in the USA."

At 4:00 a.m. on the morning of August 17, the phone rang to recall Steve to depart. He grabbed his things, gave Sharon a big hug and kiss, and was off. The obvious question was why didn't Steve marry Sharon before he left?

Several Panthers got married on short notice just before leaving for the desert. Steve thought long and hard about it. While he didn't tell Sharon, he confided in a friend that he really wanted to marry her but didn't want her to be a "war widow" if something happened. It was not an easy decision, but his mind was made up. The two never spoke about it before Steve left, yet Sharon respected the decision after hearing about it later. Besides, even if she disagreed, now was not the time to argue about it.

PART 8

The Desert

The ADVON Team

Things were happening fast. Steve would be one of the first to depart the Beach as part of the advance team, known as the ADVON team. Led by Colonel Hank Haden, the wing director of operations who had arrived at the Beach the day before Iraq invaded Kuwait, and had yet to unpack, Steve was joined by fellow pilots Chuck Fox, Danny Clifton, and Danno Swift.

Together they boarded a C-5A Galaxy and flew first to Torrejón Air Base in Spain. After a brief RON (remain overnight) in Spain, the ADVON team landed at King Fahd International Airport on August 18. King Fahd was a commercial airport under construction just northwest of Dhahran, Saudi Arabia and was only about 60 percent complete.

The tower was manned by an Air Force combat control team who had to climb 540 stairs into a tower with no air-conditioning whose temperatures eclipsed 130 degrees during the day. They found the field using radios and eyeballs only and, after landing on the runway, cleared to the first available parking spot and completely unpacked the aircraft.

At the time, the Bechtel Corporation was supervising the construction at King Fahd and quickly turned over use of all available facilities to the Panthers, including some small trailers being used by the construction workers as temporary housing. The first order of business was to survey the airfield. The control tower, runways, and ramps were done, but the airfield had no navigational aids or fuel storage and few support buildings. It had the bare necessities, but only barely.

Panthers Deploy

On August 7, 1990, the first Air Force fighters departed the states for Saudi Arabia, followed nine days later by the Panthers. The trip required two long flights, with a stopover in Europe. Thirty-two jets departed the Beach in four cells of eight to get twenty-four downrange. Each cell included two air spares, which would get plugged into the flight if any of the primary six aircraft in each cell developed refueling or mechanical problems.

Flights took off in the late afternoon, meaning the pilots would not be well-rested for the start of their fourteen-plus-hour first leg. The plan was to rejoin with the air refueling tankers over the east coast, cross the Atlantic, and all land at Morón Air Base in Spain. They would RON, then either await further instructions or continue on to King Fahd.

The deployment from Myrtle Beach to Morón was nothing short of a disaster. For starters, the flights flew through thunderstorms early on, largely the fault of the tankers. Several pilots would have to go "lost wingman," meaning they lost sight of the tanker while in the storms and had to maneuver away to avoid a potential collision—an unnerving experience out over the Atlantic. As if that weren't enough, Hendo's jet developed a serious problem.

Hendo experienced fuel fumes in the cockpit while refueling which were so strong they would virtually incapacitate him. His vision would get blurry, and he would feel nauseous; but after refueling, he would feel a little better. He was finally able to isolate the problem and vent the cabin air after each refueling, but there were times when he actually thought he would not make the deployment.

The thing that kept Hendo going was the idea that he was not going to be left behind while his squadron went off to war. This single-mindedness and focus would drive many of the Panthers to do things that they had never done before. It was not so much a matter of pride but rather the intense desire to be there with everybody else. Nobody wanted to miss out on this opportunity, whatever that opportunity might be.

Speaking of opportunity, the deployment was not a total disaster for everyone. After being told by Rick Shatzel he wasn't going, Sweet was back in the mix. When another pilot was unable to deploy because his wife was on the verge of giving birth to their first child, a replacement was needed. Just like that, Rob was now part of the deployment.

As the youngest pilot in the squadron, he was designated as the number two air spare in the fourth and final cell of A-10s, meaning that a lot of things would have to go wrong before Sweetness would be flying to Saudi in an A-10. He knew as much, so he didn't pack very well for the flight. He anticipated that following refueling, he would be returning to the Beach to board a military transport for a long, boring flight.

As luck would have it, plenty of things went wrong, and he was in. With the sun setting behind him and the east coast fading from sight, Sweetness was alone with his thoughts. One thing was for sure—he was not looking forward to the multiple in-flight refuelings over the dark Atlantic Ocean.

Rob had a total of one previous night air refueling under his belt from RTU. Now five of his newest best friends, along with the tanker crew, had all eyes on him. His first refueling hookup went smoothly, partly because he did not have enough experience to be nervous. But the second one did not turn out nearly as well, and it took him forever to get connected to the tanker. The cell flew through several thunderstorms, requiring Rob to go lost wingman once, and almost a second time, but necessity is a great teacher. Sweetness and the gang landed in Morón fifteen hours after take-off. On the bright side, he increased his total flight time in the A-10 by 15 percent in one sortie.

After shutting down the jets in Spain, the dog-ass-tired Panthers were forced to stay awake in a futile attempt to adjust their sleep cycles. Twenty-four hours later, they were again airborne. After a twelve-hour flight, they joined Steve and the ADVON team at King Fahd and got right to work.

Welcome to the Desert

The Panthers were the first combat squadron to arrive at King Fahd. Panther maintainers, who had arrived shortly before the A-10s, greeted the aircraft. As Sweetness, Hendo, and the other pilots opened their canopies, they were greeted by a blast of heat the likes of which none had felt before. It was August in the Saudi Arabian desert, and daytime temperatures routinely reached over a hundred degrees in the shade.

After parking the jets, the pilots were fed and immediately issued chemical warfare gear. Before they could unpack, Colonel Sharpe walked over and said, "We think they are coming over the fence tomorrow, and our job will be to slow them down." In unison they thought, *Welcome to the desert.*

To stop the onslaught of Iraqi mechanized and armored divisions, the A-10s would have to do battle with half a load of fuel, and armed only with the 30mm cannon, loaded with combat mix, and the Maverick missiles they brought. There were no other munitions yet on scene. But make no mistake about it, these Warthogs brought a lot of firepower to the fight.

Thin Line in the Sand

The pilots gathered for a quick intelligence update, which forecast that Saddam was about to move his forces south into Saudi Arabia. The Panthers immediately put four pilots and jets on twenty-four-hour alert and would rotate that duty among all available pilots.

Nobody knew for sure what was going to happen. Some of the pilots went to bed wearing their gas masks. It was a time when the Panthers were most vulnerable. Steve, Hendo, and two other pilots were moved into a ten-by-twenty room in one of the trailers, which would be home for the duration of the war. Steve described his feelings to Sharon in a letter he penned six days after arriving in Saudi.

```
I know that sounds strange but you can't live
your life in fear. It is difficult to describe
life here. You go from being scared to death war
is going to break out to laughing and joking like
you're back at the Beach.
```

The excitement and anticipation during those first few days was incredible. Everyone was in full go to war mode, and they thought that each day would bring Saddam's forces streaming south. Each day that passed moved the Panthers closer to fully combat ready. Fuel, ammunition, and supplies streamed into the base.

But it was a thin line in the sand, and they knew it. What they lacked in provisions they made up for in confidence tempered by the reality on the ground. The only thing standing between the Iraqi forces massed in Kuwait and major cities in Saudi Arabia were the A-10s at King Fahd and a brigade of 82nd Airborne troops in the desert.

The United States Army

Shortly after Steve's arrival at King Fahd, he drove north into the desert to discuss a basic game plan and defensive strategy with the 82nd Airborne units arrayed south of the Kuwaiti border. Steve felt it was important to have a plan with as much firepower against the invading forces, while at the same time protecting the 82nd.

The basic plan was that the 82nd was going to slow down the advancing units with the limited firepower they had, and the A-10s would provide close air support, or CAS, wherever the 82nd needed it. All knew that the best they could do was slow down the Iraqis. It was a simple plan but really the only one that these first American forces could implement under the circumstances.

Following these meetings, Steve returned back to the unit and briefed all the pilots about the game plan that the 82nd units had come up with for the defense of their portion of northeastern Saudi Arabia.

The Shield

America's initial response to Iraq's invasion of Kuwait was named Operation Desert Shield, which began by flooding American ground, naval, and air power into the Middle East. As the name implies, it started as a defensive effort. As supplies poured into King Fahd, everyone worked together at a furious pace to establish a base of operations and basic defensive fortifications.

The team began construction of a permanent operations building and filled thousands upon thousands of sandbags as protection against SCUD missile attacks. Makeshift furniture started to fill the buildings and living spaces, and a small city began to spring up, one tent at a time, in the desert.

The landscape was barren and sandy, and after flying around the local area, some noticed that the A-10 did not blend in well with its surroundings. Not surprising, since the A-10 was originally designed to destroy Soviet armor in Europe. As a result, the aircraft was painted with a dark green camouflage pattern, which was great for low-altitude employment in Europe and Korea, but not so great for the desert. The dark green paint scheme would be easier to see against both the blue skies and clouds over Iraq, but there was neither thought of nor time for repainting.

The alert aircraft, dark paint and all, flew a limited schedule for the first week while the unit dug in. As soon as it became apparent that Saddam's forces were staying put, the Panthers expanded flight operations to get all their pilots back in the air. It wasn't until the end of August that Sweetness and many of his fellow pilots would get their first flight in the theater.

During those early weeks, there was some grumbling from the pilots who felt like they were just sitting there, rotting in the desert. Pilots are only happy when they fly, no matter the circumstances. The combination of the heat, unknown threat, round-the-clock vigilance, distance from home, and lack of flying did not make for a great atmosphere.

Steve and other squadron leaders were challenged to keep the troops focused on the potential task at hand. But there was not too much complaining because, in the first few weeks following the deployment, each day could have been the day that the Iraqis came over the border, and it is this tension that left little time for other far less important distractions. Steve described the scene and his thoughts to Sharon.

```
One guy was talking about getting out, some are
just bitching about things when we do not have
it bad at all. The other thing is we have been
getting paid good money for several years to be
ready to do this and it is interesting to see
how that affects people. Do not worry, I am not
turning into Rambo, I am scared and concerned, but
my commitment gets me through. So does preparing.
```

But as days turned to weeks, it became apparent to the pilots that Saddam Hussein's forces were digging themselves in for an extended visit to Kuwait. This began the long period of wait-and-see.

Hurry Up and Wait

Hurry up and mobilize. Hurry up and deploy. Hurry up and get ready. Now wait. With the passing of each day came the realization that Saddam's forces were not coming south, and that the coalition buildup had prevented the fight that the Panthers so eagerly anticipated. Steve summed up the feelings of many in a letter home.

```
I have to keep reminding myself that I'm getting
the job done just by being here. I am not itching
for war but this sitting around is such a waste.
Still it is better than war.
```

Steve reverted to his Korea mode as soon as he landed in Saudi. Working fourteen-hour days seven days a week, he was on the job preparing. Gathering information on the capabilities of the Iraqi forces, meeting with representatives from the army, and taking in all the information he could get from CNN and any other source he could get his hands on. Steve thought it important not only to know the details but to understand the big picture as well.

Understanding this concept is one key to understanding fighter pilot mentality. Nobody really wants to go to war. The price to pay is too high. Friends are lost. The A-10, while built for survivability, was going to be operating in some very dangerous territory. Some of the pilots and planes would not be coming home. And while not one of the pilots there thought that they would not return, privately each was almost sure that not everyone would come home from this deployment.

On the other hand was the desire to fly, fight, and win. The competitive spirit fostered by the competition in pilot training, LIFT, RTU, operational units, and the fighter weapons school was a necessary element for a fighting force. The conflict between personal survival and mission accomplishment went to the core of each pilot, and each would deal with that situation in his own way when the time came.

For now, that time had not come, and the uncertainty of its arrival wore on everyone. Steve stayed calm on the outside but expressed his frustration in a letter to Sharon.

```
Now I hear that Congress is starting to cry about
Bush pushing us to war. I don't think they appre-
ciate just how fucking miserable it is over here.
The endless waiting is maddening.
```

Steve and his fellow pilots needed an outlet other than flying, but Houston, we had a problem.

General Order One

With forces flowing into the Middle East from around the world, Coalition commander General "Stormin'" Norman Schwarzkopf needed a tool to preserve the fragile coalition forming and maintain good order and discipline. Enter General Order Number One, or GO-1. The statement of military purpose and necessity of the order was clear:

```
Operation Desert Shield places United States Armed
Forces into USCENTCOM AOR countries where Islamic
law and Arabic customs prohibit or restrict
certain activities which are generally permissible
in western societies. Restrictions upon these
activities are essential to preserving U.S. host
nation relations and the combined operations of
U.S. and friendly forces.
```

Nobody in the military would question the need for GO-1, but the prohibited activities listed in section 2(c) might be a problem for fighter pilots.

```
2. Prohibited Activities:

   c. Introduction, possession, use, sale,
   transfer, manufacture, or consumption of any
   alcoholic beverage
```

Not only was GO-1 clear and widely distributed, the common belief was that getting caught with alcohol was the fastest way to wind up on a cargo flight stateside. Whatever the case, one thing was for sure: the pilots were getting ready to go to war and lay their life on the line, and perhaps not return, and were not going to be denied an occasional drink along the way. American ingenuity took care of the rest.

The Panthers found ways to bend the rule in a number of ways. First, ingenious friends and family members sent bottles of seemingly harmless liquids whose contents were replaced with the spirit of choice. Whiskey in Listerine bottles and gin with green food coloring in Scope bottles were among the favorites. Others took matters into their own hands.

American service members were supplied with alcohol-free beer, which the pilots figured they could turn into real beer by adding sugar and yeast. Some opened their bottles of beer, added the key ingredients, and closed them back up, not realizing that the fermentation process would require venting of the gases produced.

One day, they heard a loud "Oh shit!" and unmistakable sound of broken glass as bottles began exploding. In the quiet of the Saudi Arabian desert, it made a lot of noise. One brave (meaning junior) pilot was sent to rescue the surviving beers, donned in full chemical gear to prevent contamination by the concoction and injury from exploding glass. The end result of their brewing efforts was a disgusting concoction that almost no one could stomach.

The final source of liquid contraband was pallets shipped from Myrtle Beach laden with spare aircraft parts. There was always room on the pallet for a little care package that did not have to go through the usual customs inspections. Getting in alcohol or other "illegal" items ended up being more of a game than anything else.

The ultimate incentive for all of this work was not the immediate need for alcohol but rather the challenge of beating the system. It did lead to a Saturday-evening ritual where a few pilots would gather to have quiet drinks together. Quiet was the key, because it would have been a terrible mistake to draw attention to themselves in the face of the possible consequences, and they made sure these "meetings" did not interfere in any way with the serious training they were immersed in.

Desert Training

As weeks turned into months, the Panthers' training program intensified to give the pilots the knowledge and experience they might need should events heat up in the desert. Academic training focused on Iraqi capabilities, weapons employment, and threat reactions.

Steve wanted to ensure the pilots were ready to take the fight to the enemy and live to fly another day. His efforts included detailed briefings on the Warthog's self-defense capabilities, the basic understanding of which is important to this story.

Missiles designed to shoot down aircraft are sophisticated weapons. On the front end is a seeker that tracks the target using infrared (heat), radar (reflected radio-frequency energy), or electro-optics, a type of visual tracking system. The A-10 is equipped with self-protection measures against most of these systems.

The first is a jamming pod. Desert Storm A-10s carried the ALQ-131 electronic countermeasures (ECM) pod, a programmable externally mounted jamming pod designed to counter air-to-air, surface-to-air, and early warning detection radars. The pod is not magic, meaning it does not make the aircraft invisible or defeat every threat. Instead, it helps delay detection and increase the miss distance of threat radar and missile systems.

The second is expendables, countermeasures deployed from the aircraft. Chaff, a cloud of small strips of reflective metal, is designed to cause the threat radar to transfer lock from the aircraft to the metal strips ejected from the aircraft. Flares are metal-based pyrotechnic compounds ignited upon ejection from the aircraft that mimic the heat signature of the engine exhaust in an effort to decoy the infrared seeker lock from the aircraft exhaust to the flare. Electro-optical systems track in the visual spectrum, and while some can be defeated with flares, many cannot.

As a last-ditch effort, there is one more option before prayer. Engagement success requires that the missile fuse, or detonate, within the lethal radius of the warhead. If the missile blows up far enough away, damage is minimized or avoided.

Missiles have two fusing methods. The first is contact fusing. As the name applies, impact with the target sets off the contact fuse and immediate warhead detonation, also called a bad day at the office. Contact fusing turns the "miss-ile" into a "hit-tile."

The second detonation mode is proximity fusing. As the name implies, the missile fuses when it gets in the vicinity of the target. Proximity fuses emit radar or laser energy designed to detect a passing aircraft and trigger detonation as the missile passes as close to the target as the intercept geometry allows. Deploying chaff as the missile nears the aircraft can trigger the proximity fuse and cause detonation outside the lethal warhead radius.

The "last-ditch" maneuver is a combination of aggressive aircraft maneuvering and deployment of chaff and flares, again to increase missile miss distance. Of course, this only works if you can see the missile in time and have enough airspeed and altitude to maneuver. Not a pilot's favorite option, but it is better than the alternative.

Flying training included review and practice of these survival tactics, since you might not get a second chance to defeat a surface-to-air missile. As the possibility of war grew, the Panthers upped their game and shot live Mavericks and dropped live bombs. This training was complimented by academics stressing clear communication, bombing and strafe accuracy, and defensive reactions. It also included extensive review of aircraft systems, just in case something went wrong.

EPs

Training for combat included rigorous study of emergency procedures, known as EPs. EPs had been part of Steve's aviation experience starting at the Academy with soaring and T-41 and continued through pilot training, LIFT, and RTU. At the heart of EP training was an in-depth understanding of aircraft systems and strict adherence to checklist procedures. The golden rules for aircraft emergencies were the same for every single aircraft, in order of priority: aviate, navigate, and communicate.

Training for EPs in the A-10 started almost immediately in RTU and was reviewed and practiced every time Steve sat down in the cockpit trainer. More realistic EP training was accomplished in the simulator, which could replicate the cockpit indications and warning lights associated with various system problems.

The A-10 checklist contained critical emergency procedures presented in boldface capital letters that pilots had to accomplish in the published sequence without reference to the checklist. Most emergencies started with illumination of the MASTER CAUTION, an amber light mounted directly in front of the pilot. A MASTER CAUTION light indicated that the pilot needed to check other instruments and lights to identify the exact nature of the emergency. Major aircraft systems malfunctions were indicated by caution lights on a panel mounted to the bottom right corner of the instrument panel.

Steve and Rob trained together with emphasis on hydraulic, electrical, engine, and flight control problems. Typical EP training involved a single system failure or malfunction. Battle damage in combat could result in multiple EPs involving several systems, which would require both quick and thorough analysis, and near-immediate action to remedy.

EP training kept the pilots focused on flying and helped them build confidence in their ability to get the job done. One of those jobs would be combat search and rescue, where the A-10s would play a critical role in helping other coalition pilots recover from their own emergencies.

CSAR

Preparing for the possibility of armed conflict with Iraq meant hoping for the best but planning for the worse. This planning included extensive work developing a robust combat search and rescue capability, and the A-10s were at the heart of the CSAR plan. Supported by dedicated AWACS controllers and a fleet of helicopters, the Warthogs were the only dedicated coalition fixed-wing rescue asset. Their wartime tasking would include sitting CSAR alert and scrambling to assist any pilot shot down in enemy territory.

Steve knew of plans to use the A-10s for CSAR missions and needed to train up the Panthers for this role. While not an enviable job, CSAR was a tasking the A-10 community took seriously and every other fighter pilot appreciated, even if they never said so. Steve needed to teach his CSAR pilots to deal with the unique circumstances surrounding the recovery of a friendly pilot during combat operations.

Steve taught the CSAR pilots to fly with several important guidelines in mind. First, don't add to the CSAR effort by getting shot down. Second, verify there is a survivor to rescue. Third, marshal as many assets as possible to protect the downed airman. Finally, coordinate these assets to protect and recover the downed airman. Simple enough.

While a relatively simple set of rules, in practice they were exceedingly difficult to accomplish in combat. Only a select group of pilots would get trained for CSAR, and the alert missions would be led by the Panthers' most experienced CSAR pilots. Steve's experience as an LSO at Alex and CSAR pilot at Suwon were invaluable, and he shared everything the learned about rescue operations during a series of training sessions during Desert Shield.

The initial plan was to place two A-10s on CSAR alert at King Khalid Military City, a coalition air base some 250 miles west-northwest of King Fahd. Located only eighty miles from the Iraqi border and one hundred miles from the Kuwaiti border, it was perfectly positioned to support the areas most likely in need of CSAR missions. Planning and training for CSAR missions kept the Panthers focused on their work and their minds occupied with productive thoughts. Keeping that focus was a challenge in the face of so many unknowns.

The Roller Coaster Ride

The biggest problem for commanders at all levels during Desert Shield was the wait. Not knowing what was going to happen, how long they were going be there, or if they would ever see combat started impacting morale. As summer turned to fall, rumors about rotation of units into and out of the desert ran rampant. Some heard that rotations would start around Thanksgiving. Others heard Christmas. Many heard that the first units in would be the first to rotate home. After months of Spartan desert living, everyone was thinking about home.

In late 1990, word came down that the commanders in theater had decided there would be no rotation. The experience and training by the units in the desert were critical, and the people originally deployed would be there until something happened or their services were no longer needed. This decision, to some extent, helped ease the roller coaster ride.

Once everyone knew there would be no rotations, morale stabilized a bit. People understood they were there for the duration, whatever that might be. For his part, Steve stayed on an even keel through the roller coaster of emotion and excitement. His routine of hard work, and an ever-present positive outlook, helped stabilize the squadron.

Not that he didn't hear the same rumors as everyone else, it's just that he never let anybody see his own ups and downs. In letters home, he wrestled with his own feelings about the unknown wait but never complained. His tapes home were most revealing.

It's hard to believe we've been here as long as we have, in some cases; and in other cases, it doesn't seem like we've really been here that long. But we are all getting tired of just sitting around and waiting for something to happen.

It was one thing to go remote to Korea for two and a half years thinking it would be one year. That was no big deal. It's been tough here, the open-ended nature of this. To take off with just a couple of weeks' notice and not know when it is going to end has really been kind of tough.

We really don't have that much to look forward. I am almost at a point where I stop counting the days, because when you don't know what number you count to, it seems kind of pointless to count; although we are approaching the hundredth-day point here fairly shortly.

I feel like we are supporting a just cause and we are doing what needs to be done, and I guess if I were home, I'd probably be miserable, wishing I were over here.

I guess we are all kind of happy, though, that they did finally come out and say, "We are here for the duration," in that now the daily rotation rumors have stopped flying which will really put this on an emotional yo-yo. Now the yo-yo basically has had the string cut, we're all rolling across the floor. But at least we know what we are up against.

Supporting a just cause and doing what needs to be done were echoes from Vice President Bush's commencement speech, President Bush's messages to the nation, and Steve's sense of duty. He was committed to seeing this through and was steadied by his constant letter writing.

Shā Shā La Rué

Steve wrote letters home to help pass the time. And not just a few letters. Lots of letters. Family, friends, and even strangers got letters from Steve. Most of all, he wrote to Sharon. During his six months in the desert, he hand-wrote her some eighty-five letters filling over 275 pages with his thoughts, hopes, fears, desires, frustrations, and plans for their future. One of Sharon's pet names was Shā Shā La Rué.

Shā Shā responded in kind with almost daily cards and letters. Writing was their way to not only stay connected, but to grow their relationship. They wrote about everything under the sun, but the one thing you could count on in every single letter was some expression of their love for each other.

```
I really do love you and look forward to becoming
husband and wife. I am glad I waited for you.
Despite being over here, I am the luckiest man
alive knowing that I am engaged to you.

Your letters are still the highlight point of my
day. They choke me up when I saw "the future Mrs.
Sharon Phillis" I mean I think about being married
```

a lot, and I like the thought. Seeing that in writing really hit me.

I still feel lucky to have you and love you with all my heart. Knowing that this will be over and that we have the rest of our lives together gives me so much to look forward to. It makes this more bearable. I miss you and love you and hope I can see you soon.

I don't know how I survived 30 years without you. After one short year I can't imagine life without you. Even the separation I feel like we are doing together. I don't face what is happening alone and that makes you stronger. It makes this ordeal bearable. I also wish I could be there for our anniversary, but I take comfort knowing that we will have many more together.

I don't know what to say, but it is difficult to stop writing. I miss you and writing makes me feel closer to you. I have already made up my mind and you had to know. My life has been so much more enjoyable, I can't imagine my life without you. I know this separation is difficult, but having you to endure that with me helps out a lot. I miss you very much, I love you and as soon as they let me I'm going to come looking for you.

I don't deserve you. I don't know why you stick by me, but I'm awful glad you do. Honey I was afraid that all this time apart would stagnate the relationship. I feel just like you that our relationship continues to grow. I feel better about us every day. People are supposed to be nervous about getting married but I am not.

I can't imagine or even picture my life without you being a part of it. You're stuck with it. I am hopelessly ensnared in Sha Sha La Rue's web love. Thank God.

I don't feel like I exist as an individual
anymore. I feel like Steve Phillis doesn't exist
anymore. He has been replaced by Steve Phillis/
Sharon Taflan, the cutest couple in the world. I
guess that is why this deployment is so difficult.
I am separated from the best part of me and I have
been for too long, far too long. Your card says
it all. It doesn't seem possible, but even though
I haven't seen you for over four months I still
feel closer to you that I ever have before. Honey
I guess you're going to have to face it. We are in
love. Thank God.

Never has anyone captured my heart as you have.
I guess it is because I know I am loved. The fact
you return my love and make me feel love. I never
had it so good. I have to keep reminding myself
that the separation will pass. That when compared
to all the years we will have together this time
will be a small part. Even though it seems like
an eternity now. It gets harder each day. Sharon
I don't have much to offer but if you will have
me, I am yours. Forever. But the best thing that
has ever happened to me was the night on the beach
when you said you would be my wife. You made me
the luckiest man alive.

Sharon wrote many of the same feelings back to Steve, and
letter writing helped her cope with the separation.

Each day that passes I miss you but I also realize
just how much you mean to me. Even though you are
eons away with your letters you can still make me
smile and feel good inside. I love you more and
more each day and I just keep going knowing that I
will be able to spend the rest of my living years
with the most wonderful man on the earth- That's
you do do head!

I am happy just knowing we have a unique love that most people never find. We are lucky, it took a while but I wouldn't change a thing. Steve, please just remember that I love you and no matter what happens or how long it takes to come home, when you do get back to Myrtle Beach I'll be here for you, now and always.

Steve you mean so much to me - sometimes I am really frightened what is going on over there and I don't want anything to happen - I love you too much and we will be together someday and for the rest of our lives. I keep the faith and prayers and hopes for you every day. You are my everything and I want us to be a husband and wife forever.

I just want you to come home so we can start our life together. I want to be Mrs. Phillis. I want to hold you and never, ever let you go. I keep hoping that this will not last too much longer but, no matter how long it takes I will be waiting for you. I love you so much and I can't imagine my life without you being a part of it.

Steve, you mean so much to me. I never thought I could love someone as much as I do you and every day it just keeps growing. It is such a good feeling to know that we do love each other. Our relationship has all the wonderful qualities of trust, honor, respect, and lust, oh I mean love. No, I do lust after you too.

At times she was so inspired she wrote Steve a poem.

You're in my heart
    And in my dreams
You're on my mind
    And it's plain to see
You're the man I love
    Who was sent to me

```
You're a gift from above
    That I thank for endlessly
You're everything I wanted
    And I wouldn't ask for more
You're the man I love
    And I will always adore
I look at the stars every night
    And thinking of you
I make that special wish
    That soon I'll be your wife
I will always be faithful
    And true to you
I will love you forever
    And be eternally grateful
        I love you Steve - Always!
            Love upon love,
                Sharon XOXO
```

Support from Home

Support from home was strong, and important to everyone over in the desert. As busy as he was, Steve made time to stay connected with America. Early in Desert Shield, he was adopted by a fourth-grade class in Novi, Michigan. An article entitled, "Letters to the Homefront, Air Force Capt. Writes to Novi Woods Elementary Students," was published in the *Novi News* on December 3, 1990.

```
His Air Force buddies call him "Warthog," but to
24 students at Novi Woods Elementary School Capt.
Steve Phillis is not as belligerent as the name
implies.
```

```
Phillis, endeared to Sally Chandler's fourth-
grade class for his love of the Teenage Mutant
Ninja Turtles, has a dad who used to work on the
railroad, has a fiancée he plans to marry on his
return from Saudi Arabia (also a Mutant Turtle
fan), and has a lot of time on his hands.
```

The class has written to Phillis at least five times, sending candy, pictures and a holiday tape. Their first letter was mailed the first week of the school year.

Phillis recently responded with a personal, hand-written letter to each student. He did not send 24 identical letters. Phillis wrote 24 different letters, one for each student in Chandler's class.

Chandler wanted to have her class write to a soldier in Saudi Arabia, but she did not want just any soldier. Chandler wanted to know who her class would be writing to, so she would be certain he or she would write back.

Phillis did answer the class, but to have him answer every student individually was an unexpected bonus.

When the conflict in the Middle East is over, or when Phillis is permitted to leave Saudi Arabia, he will come to visit the class, Chandler said.

"He was one of the first troops over there so he's been there for quite some time," Chandler said.

For Steve's part, it was a labor of love and a way to stay connected and grounded. When he heard about the newspaper article, he told his family about it in a tape.

A fourth-grade class kind of adopted me, and would write me letters, so I wrote each one of the kids an individual letter back, which I guess shocked everybody. The kids got such a kick out of it. The teacher was so impressed that she called the local paper, and they had a picture of the kids, I guess with their letters, which appeared on the front page, and they had a nice article about me and Sharon.

I've gotten two more stacks of letters from the kids. Haven't had a chance to read them and answer them, but I am going to try to get that done this week. I think what I am going to do this time is write down each kid's name and say something about what they said in the letter and write one letter back and try to mention all their names because it was just too much for me to write thirty-some-odd individual letters, I ended up staying up all night.

Sally Chandler's fourth-grade class kept up their letter writing, and Steve responded with one long letter back. He also got a wonderful letter from his mom, which he told Sharon about.

Got a letter from Mom today. She really likes you. She said and I quote "it may have taken you a little longer than the others to find the right marriage partner, but when you did you really found the gem. She's a wonderful girl and I am glad you stumbled into each other."

Steve was delighted to get his mother's support. Sharon also let Steve know about all the support he and his fellow troops were enjoying back home.

January 24, 1991

Honey, you are all supported here in the states. They can't keep enough flags in the stores, they are back ordering them too.

When he wasn't reading or writing letters, Steve kept a close eye on world events generally and his commander in chief specifically.

President Bush

On September 11, 1990, President Bush addressed a joint session of Congress to update the nation on events in the Persian Gulf.

Everyone deployed to the desert with access to a television tuned in to listen to the president.

At this moment, our brave servicemen and women stand watch in that distant desert and on distant seas, side by side with the forces of more than twenty other nations. They are some of the finest men and women of the United States of America. And they're doing one terrific job. These valiant Americans were ready at a moment's notice to leave their spouses and their children, to serve on the front line halfway around the world. They remind us who keeps America strong: they do. In the trying circumstances of the Gulf, the morale of our service men and women is excellent. In the face of danger, they're brave, they're well trained, and dedicated.

A soldier, Private First Class Wade Merritt of Knoxville, Tennessee, now stationed in Saudi Arabia, wrote his parents of his worries, his love of family, and his hope for peace. But Wade also wrote, "I am proud of my country and its firm stance against inhumane aggression. I am proud of my army and its men. I am proud to serve my country." Well, let me just say, Wade, America is proud of you and is grateful to every soldier, sailor, marine, and airman serving the cause of peace in the Persian Gulf. I also want to thank the chairman of the Joint Chiefs of Staff, General Powell; the chiefs here tonight; our commander in the Persian Gulf, General Schwarzkopf; and the men and women of the Department of Defense. What a magnificent job you all are doing. And thank you very, very much from a grateful people. I wish I could say that their work is done. But we all know it's not.

So, if there ever was a time to put country before self and patriotism before party, the time is now. And let me thank all Americans, especially those here in this chamber tonight, for your support for our armed forces and for their mission. That support will be even more important in the days to come. So, tonight I want to talk to you about what's at stake—what we must do together to defend civilized values around the world and maintain our economic strength at home.

Our objectives in the Persian Gulf are clear, our goals defined and familiar: Iraq must withdraw from Kuwait completely, immediately, and without condition. Kuwait's legitimate government must be restored. The security and stability of the Persian Gulf must be assured. And American citizens abroad must be protected. These goals are not ours alone. They've been endorsed by the United Nations Security Council five times in as many weeks. Most countries share our concern for principle. And many have a stake in the stability of the Persian Gulf. This is not, as Saddam Hussein would have it, the United States against Iraq. It is Iraq against the world.

The next day, Steve wrote Sharon about this impact of the president's words.

The highlight of the day was being told that President Bush mentioned us in his speech and appreciated the sacrifices we and our families are making. He said we were accomplishing our mission and he was proud of us. We all needed a lift and that helped me anyway.

Two months later, President Bush shared a Thanksgiving Day message to all American troops.

As we gather together for Thanksgiving this year, America has much to be truly grateful for. To those of you who are spending this holiday away from your loved ones to defend our nation's security and that of our allies, I am deeply grateful. To those of you on duty in the Persian Gulf, I say a special thank you.

Recent events prove the world is still a dangerous and unstable place. Along with the triumph of freedom around the world comes new challenges, especially in the Middle East. Once again, you, the men and women of our Armed Forces, have responded to the call of duty to protect freedom and stand firm against aggression. And

*once again, you have the full support of the American people and
the thanks of this president.*

*You know, Barbara and I have spent a lot of Thanksgivings
with a family we're proud of. Well, this year is no different, as we
spend Thanksgiving in the Persian Gulf. And as Americans celebrate this special day back home, know that you are in their hearts.
America is proud of you and the job you're doing. Almost two years
ago, I began my inaugural address with a prayer, seeking God's
wisdom and guidance in all that we face. Earlier this month, with
American troops facing down aggression overseas, I asked the
nation to join me in prayer, a prayer for the brave service men
and women in whom we entrust the future of this country—as
well as for those Americans held hostage. Now, this Thanksgiving,
I hope that all Americans of all faiths and walks of life will bow
their heads in appreciation for God's power to protect us and His
wisdom to guide us.*

*As members of our Armed Forces worldwide, your strength
and readiness allow the flames of freedom and democracy to
glow brightly. You represent America's best—the world's best
hope for the future. No matter where you are, I hope you're safe
and well. The entire Bush family wishes you and your family a
happy Thanksgiving. May God bless you and bring you home
safely and soon.*

The more Steve heard the president speak, the more he liked
what he heard. He picked up his tape recorder and sent his parents a tape explaining exactly how he felt.

*George Bush is a fighter pilot, he flew Navy fighters in WWII, and
he has as good as appreciation as anybody of what he is asking us
to do, so if war comes, he'll know exactly what he's asking of us.
He's taken a lot of heat in the press, but he is agonizing over this as
much as anybody, and it's really easy to sit back and second-guess*

the man who's not been at the job more than two years and is facing a tremendous world crisis that we haven't seen in a long time.

I wish Sam Nunn and the others would support him more, and hack at him less, because I really think that if he had the right to support at home there's not a whole lot he couldn't do.

I think he believes in us, and I believe in him. I really don't think we are going to have too much to worry about. I think things are going to be done right, so if it does come down to war, most of us are gonna come home. It is not a cheerful thought, but I actually feel pretty good about how things are going on.

Steve was proud of his president, the cause he was supporting, and his country.

Proud to be an American

Lee Greenwood's song "Proud to Be an American" was the Gulf War's anthem. It was heard all across America and overseas anywhere Americans were stationed. Steve loved the song and played it all the time. The lyrics expressed many of the patriotic feelings Steve felt since childhood, and the songmeister often sang along when the song was played.

The song is about taking pride in being an American, understanding that freedom is a gift earned by the sacrifice of our servicemembers, and that freedom is worth fighting for. The last line few words were Steve's rallying cry, "God Bless the U.S.A."

God bless indeed. Steve told Sharon, "Lee Greenwood's music will always bring a big smile to my face and a small tear to my eye." The last words of Lee's song were a reminder of the role faith played in Steve's life.

Faith

Steve took stock of his faith as he thought about the possibility of war. His views on religion had changed at the Academy because there was a conflict between his spiritual belief and his desire, as a budding scientist, to have proof of the things in the world around him. Still, be believed in God and the role God played in his life, especially as it related to Sharon.

Steve held onto his faith in the desert and wrote to Sharon about their wedding plans.

```
I don't want a Catholic wedding. I'm not devout
and the hassle with you not being Catholic isn't
worth it.

I would like us to pick the minister together
though as I think that is the most important
decision. I may want a priest from back home to
participate. Father Mirabelli was very important
to me growing up, and it would mean a lot if
he could participate. How do you feel about us
picking out the scripture readings?
```

In several letters, he thanked God for bringing Sharon into his life, but for the most part kept his feelings on faith to himself while he prepared the squadron for combat.

High Altitude Hogs

In late 1990, the Panthers got word they would be fighting a "high war," meaning that the low-altitude "bread and butter" tactics practiced stateside would give way to higher-altitude attacks. Steve was part of the team that recommended this approach and knew it to be more survivable given the threat.

Intelligence assessments of the Iraqi army revealed their forces were well equipped with anti-aircraft artillery (AAA) and man portable surface-to-air missiles (MANPADS). The sheer number of guns and MANPADS would make low-altitude employment extremely hazardous. While Iraq's medium- and high-altitude SAM coverage was nothing to sneeze at, it paled in comparison to the low-altitude threat.

Now, high altitude is a matter of perspective. To most hog drivers at the time, anything above a thousand feet was high attitude. High altitude in the desert meant the A-10s would fly in the fifteen- to twenty-five-thousand-foot range and employ ordnance above a ten-thousand-foot floor. Steve's experience at Suwon provided invaluable in preparing the Panthers for a high war.

The first order of business was to practice high-altitude delivery of free-fall, or non-precision, weapons. Training required precise airspeed and dive angle control to reduce errors, but the lack of a computer-generated bombsite or wind-corrected attack display meant free-fall weapons would not offer a precision strike option, even in the hands of a highly experienced pilot.

Precision attack was available thanks to the Maverick missile. The AGM-65 Maverick carried by Desert Storm A-10s for daylight attacks used electro-optical (EO) television guidance. While captive on the wing, the EO Maverick's television sensor was wired to a cockpit TV monitor system, allowing the pilot to "see" what the Maverick was looking at.

The pilot could slew (steer) the TV seeker to look for targets and zoom in for a closer look. In fact, the desert hogs developed a use for this weapon probably not envisioned by its designers. Pilots used the Mavericks to help them identify targets at distance since the video images could be magnified. Of course, once the Mavericks were fired, there went the nifty search and aiming system. While a great weapon, the missile needed a distinct visual contrast for effective missile tracking, sometimes a problem in the bright desert sun, especially in the early morning and late afternoon.

Training for gun employment was not as critical for two reasons. First, the pilots had a lot of experience shooting the gun. Second, the gun would not be the primary weapon for high-altitude attacks. Nevertheless, Steve made sure his Panthers were well-trained for a "high war" and was rewarded with a new position of responsibility in the squadron.

Flight Commander

On December 1, Steve was moved out of the weapons shop and promoted to C Flight commander. As flight commander, he was in charge of the care, feeding, training, scheduling, and overall welfare of some ten pilots. C Flight pilots had a range of experience, from thousand-hour hog drivers to the squadron's newest mission-ready pilot, Sweetness.

Steve brought a new approach to the C Flight commander job, and Sweetness saw a night-and-day difference once he took over. While some flight commanders didn't really feel like they were commanding their flight, Steve took the command function of his new position seriously, as evidenced by how he talked about it in a tape sent home before Christmas.

On the first of December, I took over as the new C Flight commander, so it has been really busy. Now I am in charge of about ten guys, and I am their flight commander. I schedule them, so I try to deal with all their problems, and also try and keep them as prepared as I can, or finish up their preparation for a war. So it's been a pretty big responsibility, but it has been really great.

I wasn't sure this opportunity was going to come, and now I am real happy that I did finally get this opportunity. I've got just a great group of guys. So it has been really exciting in the last two weeks. When I first came to the Panthers I started out in C Flight. It feels kind of good to be in the C Flight again because I kind of float around from flight to flight.

But it has kept me busy. It has made my days longer. And I realize too that I can continue to overwork if I'm not careful, so I am going to have to start slacking off a little bit, giving myself some down time. I haven't really taken a day off in the last two weeks.

He also shared his excitement with Sharon over the course of several letters starting in late November.

November 22, 1990

Well now for the big news. By the time you get this it will be official. In the next couple of days Lt Col Shatzel is going to announce that I am going to take over from Major Doug Owens as the new C flight commander. I can't tell you how excited I am. This is a big step up for me and it is an unbelievable opportunity. The chance to command, especially in light of the current situation, is a tremendous opportunity.

What that means is I need your help keeping up with the families of my guys. Especially if they need anything. Eventually I will send you a list of names so you will know who the wives/girl-friends are. Don't worry, I am not asking you to do any "wives club" bullshit. And I never will.

It's just that these guys are now my responsi-bility and if they need time, or squadron help with the situation back home I've got to know. It could be the difference between whether or not all our guys get home okay.

I know this is asking a lot. I hope you under-stand. I wish I could have had more time to tell you, prepare you for this. It happened kind of fast. The kind of thing I am talking about is like when Mary Gilbert, her husband was my flight commander, called to let you know that I arrived here okay. It is another one of the liabilities hooking up with the Air Force officer. I hope that shortly after your birthday we will end this. Hopefully peacefully.

November 28, 1990

Well honey, believe it or not it finally happened.
They finally announced that I am taking over
C flight effective Saturday. Everybody seemed
shocked and pleasantly surprised. I had a long
talk with Major Owens about the flight, and talked
to the lieutenants about job responsibilities,
etc. It will be interesting to see how things go.
My approach to the job is a lot different than
the other three so I expect some growing pains.
I intend to be diplomatic but true to what I
believe. I am the only one who has always been a
fighter pilot so my perspective is different.

I am really excited. As the day approaches to take
over I get more pumped. I can't wait. I love you
and rest assured that I am being careful so that I
can come back to you safe and sound.

December 3, 1990

I hate to say this but I love being flight
commander. I hope I can make a difference for these
guys. I had a meeting with my flight today . . .
You know the drill . . . There is a new sheriff in
town and his name is Reggie Hammond. I think it
went well.

December 4, 1990

Being a flight commander keeps me busy, but I
really enjoy it. It is tough though because the
other three have been flight commanders longer but
are junior in experience. We need to change a lot
of things, but I don't want to sound like a know
it all. Yes I am trying to play nice, but it is
difficult. I am biting my tongue a lot lately.

I am trying to fly with all my guys and get a feel
for how they are doing. So far it seems like they
are all pretty strong.

For some it might seem curious because responsibility for ten pilots was hardly a monumental command position. But Steve felt more of an obligation to enforce the rules based on his new-found command position, and key to that responsibility was his deeply ingrained commitment to leadership by example.

As flight commander, he reviewed all the rules he was now responsible for enforcing. His due diligence included a review of GO-1, and the language in section 5 now had a whole new meaning to him.

5. Unit Commander Responsibility: Unit Commanders and supervisors are charged to ensure all, repeat all, personnel are briefed on the prohibitions and requirements of this general order. Commanders and supervisors are expected to exercise discretion and good judgment in enforcing this general order.

Now it was his job to more closely follow the company line. That's just the way he did things, and those that knew him admired and respected him for it.

As usual, the Saturday evening social event was held in Steve's room, but his discomfort in participation meant that he often chose not to drink. He would just hop in his bunk and go to bed, soothed by the fact that if you are asleep, you are not participating or actively condoning the event. He slept better because of it and needed the rest to make some of the difficult decisions needed as C Flight commander.

Combat Pairs

As Christmas approached, word filtered down that things were starting to get more serious. Each flight commander was required to make combat pairings, selecting pilots who would fight together in two-ship elements throughout the war. Since Steve was the most experienced pilot in C Flight, it was only natural for him to combat pair with the least experienced wingman, and thus was born the two-ship of Phillis and Sweet.

Syph and Sweetness would be paired together as lead and wingman for all future combat operations. The goal of combat pairing was to get the most experience possible between the two pilots paired. At this point, Syph started to call Sweetness, "Saddam Hussein's worst nightmare," a name Syph would use throughout the war. He also asked Sharon for help to make sure Rob's girlfriend was taken care of.

> If you could do me a favor, Rob Sweet is a single guy in the flight and he has a girlfriend. Her name is Christy Sommerville. Could you give her a call and introduce yourself and try to keep her posted on what is happening especially if they do cut off the commercial phone lines? It will mean a lot to Rob to know that she won't be left in the dark. It will probably help her to know others are separated too.

It was at this point that Sweet first realized that Steve wasn't the complete hard-ass that he thought, and a series of decisions Steve made about leadership of the flight impressed Sweet—no small task as most fighter pilots are difficult to impress, and new wingmen almost impossible to impress because they don't know any better.

Syph and Sweetness began flying together right away. As a combat pair, they learned each other's tendencies and preferences. They spent extra time briefing and debriefing. Steve needed to teach Rob everything he could, because once the fighting started, they might get too busy to do much teaching, and neither wanted to learn lessons the hard way.

Prelude to War

In late November, the U.N. Security Council passed Resolution 678, requiring Iraq to withdraw from Kuwait before January 15,

1991 or face military action. At long last, the coalition had drawn a line in the sand, which gave everyone a date to look forward to. It became a planning date for many, and for those at home perhaps hope for the beginning of the end.

The arrival of December got Steve thinking about the possibility of war, and he minced no words in his letter to Sharon.

Hussein doesn't have any qualms about screwing his own people either. He is a survivor and I don't think he wants to fight. I am not sure how to interpret his latest words. I have not given up on peace, but I don't think waiting beyond January 15 is wise.

If he isn't out by then I think we should go to war. I am not looking forward to that. But when I think about that pregnant Kuwaiti female being bayoneted by an Iraqi soldier I really get mad. I don't believe he should be given more time after January 15. He is releasing hostages now, and that makes me hope for peace.

If he doesn't leave know I am ready to start shooting. I won't like it, but this cause is worth fighting for. I study a lot and fly hard now to make sure that I am ready. After all I have to make sure that I come home to you. I wish I knew what was going to happen but either way I am coming home to you as soon as I can. I don't think it will be much longer. The world will not let this go on.

Just before Christmas, Steve wrote Sharon with an update.

I don't like saying this, but Hussein is making no moves out of Kuwait and war is starting to look like the only alternative. It is hard to imagine as today seems like any other day. I wonder what it will be like the first day of war. When I wake up. I also wonder what the first combat sortie

will be like. I feel like before my first boxing
match. It isn't bad after the first punch, but
waiting for is agonizing. Hopefully it will be
over quickly. I really can't see it taking more
than a month. Keep your fingers crossed that I am
home for my birthday.

It is only 23 days until January 16 and we are
all counting the days. We/I want to get this over
and waiting is getting old. One way or the other
we will all feel better when January 15 comes and
goes. Rest assured though that I will be careful.

After the New Year, Secretary of State James Baker met with
Iraq's Foreign Minister Tariq Aziz in Geneva. Before this and
every subsequent high-level meeting, CNN paraded out experts
who invariably opined the upcoming meeting would resolve the
standoff. Sometime after each meeting, reports would surface
that no resolution was reached. Sharon kept Steve up to date on
her thoughts.

January 9, 1991

Well, I guess I'll tell you that they had a
conference in Geneva today and it didn't go well
at all. Everyone is really getting worried now.
I don't know what to think. I just know that you
are coming back to me, no matter what happens!
Just remember that! You and everyone have a lot
of support.

Each meeting raised the hopes of the Panthers, and their families, only to come crashing down to earth. Then it was United
Nations Secretary-General Javier Pérez de Cuéllar's turn, followed by Soviet special envoy Yevgeny Primakov, and finally
Soviet President Mikhail Gorbachev. The ups and downs of each
meeting raced an emotional roller coaster through the squadron,
fueled by the twenty-four-hour news cycle.

Steve watched this unfold like everyone else and sent a tape home to explain his view.

Two days ago, or wherever it was, we heard that Baker and Aziz were meeting for three times as long as they were supposed to. We were all waiting for the news report and got our hopes up that this would be solved peacefully. It was quite an emotional letdown when we listened to Baker's interview afterwards. I must admit that I was shocked. There has been a lot more posturing lately, and it will be interesting to see how this falls out.

Interesting indeed. As each meeting came and went, the calendar marched on toward the United Nations deadline of January 15. Since hope is not a strategy, the coalition continued preparations for war.

A Visit from the Boss

On January 13, the unit was visited by Brigadier General Buster Glosson, director of operations of the coalition air forces and the man in charge of the pending air campaign. Glosson gathered the pilots and told them, "The worst thing that happened in Vietnam is that we never knew what was going on. We are not going to let that happen here."

Buster proceeded to tell the pilots the overall strategy for the pending air campaign, including their anticipated role. It was a move unprecedented in the Air Force, and one that went a long way in cementing the pilots' confidence in their command leadership and the task that lay ahead.

General Glosson finished with, "Here's what we are going to do, and there's nothing that Saddam can do about it." His confidence in both the plan and the men who would carry it out was supreme. If nothing else, Glosson was absolutely certain his pilots would get the job done.

Dangerous Work and Last Letters

The most dangerous scenario for the coalition, especially early, was a large-scale Iraqi armored invasion of Saudi Arabia. The tank-killing A-10 was a critical cog in the coalition's defensive machine, so the Air Force amassed 144 Warthogs in the desert. Plans called for the A-10s to attack radar sites, surface-to-air missile batteries, and entrenched armored and mechanized divisions. All of these targets were valuable to the Iraqis, so they would be well defended.

The A-10s would be tasked with some of most dangerous missions, yet there was not a single hog pilot to be found who thought they would be shot down if hostilities broke out. The problem was that a number of "experts" opined that the aircraft attrition rate would be somewhere between 10 and 25 percent, or two to six per squadron. Everyone expected losses, even if everyone thought it would be somebody else.

Steve knew the Panthers' work would get even more dangerous during the ground war. As the weapons officer, he was one of the few Panthers privy to the details of the invasion plans. He knew the coalition was going to fake the launch of a massive ground campaign straight into Kuwait while the main assault force executed a daring left hook to outflank and encircle the Iraqi forces in and around Kuwait.

Once the ground war started, the A-10s would provide low-altitude close air support to the advancing coalition forces. The speed of the maneuver and sheer size of the effort would provide a lot of targets, but a lot of threats as well. He knew the Panthers would do their part, but also knew that every single survival feature built into and bolted onto the A-10 would be tested.

Steve, for his part, knew he too would be tested. As the tactical heart and soul of the Panthers, their success or failure would be his. It was a feeling every single weapons officer thought about at least once. As a pilot, he was supremely confident, and rightly so. So confident, in fact, that while some wrote a "last letter" home to be sent only if they did not return, Steve made no time for that. He was too busy getting ready to fight.

Thoughts from Home

Back at the Beach, Sharon's last few letters before the war expressed the sentiments of many with loved ones in the Persian Gulf.

> January 11, 1991
>
> How are you doing and are you holding up okay? I think we are all just waiting for January 15 but I think your perspective of that day is a little different than mine.
>
> You have a little more at stake but I know you are excellent at what you do and you <u>will</u> be careful and you will be back so we can be married and start our life together. Do you understand? Good!
>
> January 14, 1991
>
> I don't know what to say right now. Just know that I love you very much and I will be here for you - always!
>
> Sweetheart, yes, I am frightened but I have a lot of support from this and I want you to know that we are going to be just fine.

A Just Cause

Steve followed the news closely and had plenty of time to think about why he was in the desert and what he might be called on to do. He wrote to Sharon so that she'd know exactly how he felt.

```
I glad that I am part of this. It is what I signed
up to do and it is a just cause. I just wish that
my life's calling didn't cause us to be geographi-
cally separated. I love you honey. I will get home
when I can.
```

On January 13, 1991, Steve recorded his final tape of Desert Shield. He was upbeat, concerned about Sharon, and happy with his leaders and support from home. Near the end of the recording, he summed up exactly how he felt on the eve of Desert Storm.

I hope that whatever the Soviets and de Cuéllar have cooked up works out. Nobody wants a war, although I am going to war, if we do, for a just cause. It is something that needs to be done.

We are all hoping that we will be able to come to some kind of agreement that this can be settled peacefully but, but after what happened last week with Baker and Aziz, I seriously doubt that's going to happen.

If it does come to war though, we are extremely well trained and extremely well lead, and I believe with every fiber of my being that this will be over very quickly; and I also believe that once it is over that we are going to get the hell out of here as fast as we can— which is good for all of us.

While he was willing to sharing his feelings with his family, the same was not completely true with his fellow Panthers.

The Great Unknown

The pilots didn't share with each other many of their thoughts about pending combat. It was something they were thinking about, but a subject they kept to themselves, or perhaps shared with family and friends back home. Steve sent a tape home to explain his feelings.

Obviously, as January approaches, there's more apprehension, but, so far, we are still far enough away that things are still pretty calm. I imagine the tempo will pick up though once the New Year starts. It just seems like every day is like the first. We all keep waking up wondering what's gonna happen, and every day is the same. It's just becoming very monotonous.

Unfortunately, I think the monotony is going to change soon, but for right now, at least, the monotony is good. We all say it's kind of boring, but, in a way, we are all kind of glad it is. Nobody really wants to run away to war.

We all have wondered what war would be like, and you wonder a lot more about it now. We all have kinda the same thoughts that you really can't admit to each other about being scared, but I guess it's a natural thing. I let my people know that if you're not scared, you shouldn't be flying because you then obviously don't under-stand the situation.

Steve also wanted Sharon to know he was ready and wrote to her on January 11, 1991.

```
We are all making the final preparations for war.
It still doesn't seem real. I guess it won't seem
real until it happens. I wonder what it will be
like. I try to fly today, as I have for the last
month, just like I plan to in war. I think we have
our act together. The sortie went well. I feel as
good as you can I guess until you actually face
it. I hope it doesn't take very long, but I don't
see how it can. I think we will overwhelm them.
```

Most thoughts turned to whether something had been omitted from the planning, or if there was something more each could do to better prepare. The fear of screwing up was a lot greater than the fear of being shot down. The fighter pilot aura of invincibility would not shrink on the eve of war.

Getting Real

It got real really fast. As soon as it became clear that Saddam Hussein was not going to comply with United Nations Security Council Resolution 678 and withdraw from Kuwait, the military machine assembled sprang to life, ready to use "all necessary means" to force Iraq out of Kuwait.

The Panthers immediately started final preparations for war, and few had any idea of what to expect. Only the most senior pilots had any combat experience, because the air war in Vietnam had ended some sixteen years earlier. As a result, many of the finishing touches were first-time events for the pilots and maintainers.

The aircraft were reconfigured for combat. Radar warning receivers, jamming pods, and secure radios were reprogrammed to wartime settings. Live weapons were hung, and every gun was loaded with 1,174 rounds of combat mix consisting of five Armor Piercing Incendiary (API) rounds for every High Explosive Incendiary (HEI) round loaded.

The personal locator beacon function of the ejection seats was switched from automatic to manual, to ensure that the beacon could not be used by the Iraqis to locate downed pilots. Given the projected losses, this was an important move. Given that fact that the A-10 would be in the middle of the most dangerous action, it was especially important to the Panthers.

The pilots were also issued additional equipment, some of which they'd seen before, some they had not. Holstered in the survival vest was the pilot's service weapon, a .38 caliber aircrew revolver. The weapon was notoriously inaccurate at distance, and given this fact, most pilots planned to use it to hunt small game in a survival situation and nothing more. But when the weapon was issued, along with ammunition, it was a clear signal that "go time" was near.

Even more sobering was the issue of the EVC NH-38C Evasion Chart covering Iraq, Kuwait, and Saudi Arabia. The Evasion Chart was for use by downed pilots for several purposes. First and most obviously, it was a map used to evade capture, containing details about the terrain and available cover. Second, the chart contained a wealth of information on local plants, animals, insects, first aid, and survival techniques. Finally, the chart contained a long list of additional uses for the map, including water collection, as a blanket, and even to splint a broken bone or plug a sucking chest wound. Though many pilots had seen training versions of the Evasion Chart, most were setting their eyes on the EVC NH-38C for the first time.

Taken together, the rush of new activity brought an excitement to the squadron but also a large dose of reality that things were about to change in way that few had ever experienced. As always, Steve took it in stride and remained cool as a cucumber, at least on the outside.

Facing Reality

With General Glosson's visit just days before the start of air operations, the pilots were keyed up. They were also able to watch the political situation unfold on CNN, including the last-ditch efforts by the Russians to avert offensive air operations. It did not distract the pilots from the pending task at hand, because they had watched this type of political maneuvering for almost half a year by now. But all signs were that the big show was about to begin.

The reality of war struck each pilot differently. Some wrote home. Others talked with their fellow pilots. Still others found a quiet place and time to gather their thoughts. Most pilots, and almost all experienced pilots, had known the loss of a friend in an aircraft crash. Steve thought about his friend Donn McCorkindale.

Final Preparations

On January 14, Sandy Sharpe gathered the entire team at King Fahd to deliver a brief yet powerful speech:

> Buster Glosson, the 14th Air Division commander,
> was here yesterday. He shared with us the plan.
> It is an awesome plan. It is the largest aerial
> campaign in the history of aviation. We have
> a warm fuzzy feeling. Saddam should have wet
> britches right now. That bodes well for us here on
> the ground, the Fahd squad is well protected and
> ready for the job that needs to be done.
>
> You can look around in the five months we've been
> here and just see for yourself how ready we are.
> There is pride, professionalism that indicates
> that readiness is our profession, and we need to
> keep that in the back of our minds. There is abso-
> lutely nothing that he can do to us that we have
> not prepared for, and if we keep our wits about
> us, keep our professionalism about us, we have
> absolutely nothing to fear. I firmly believe that.
>
> General Glosson looked at the pilots eye-to-eye
> yesterday, as I am looking into your eyes today,
> and say to you when this thing is over I want to
> see every single face that I see now. We can do
> that. We have the air power both offensively and
> defensively to ensure that each and every one of
> us can go through this thing and be standing here
> to talk about it when it's over. It is going to be
> swift, sure, and decisive. I think we are very,
> very ready.
>
> I will leave you with this one thought that General
> Glosson left with us yesterday. He said that "the
> pride, honor, and dignity of the United States
> of America rests upon our shoulders right this
> moment." That is what our task is. I feel, Dave

```
feels, every single person that's come through here
to visit us feels that we are ready to uphold that
pride, honor, and dignity. I think we're going to
kick his bloody ass. Let's go do it!
```

The room erupted in enthusiastic applause, and when the ruckus died down, the team quickly returned to their final preparations.

On the eve of war when most fighter pilots were thinking about their first combat mission, Steve was thinking about Sharon. On January 16, he wrote to her.

```
I lay awake at night thinking of you and my first
night home. That always makes me smile. Knowing
that you will be with me for the rest of my life
is a great comfort. We have so many days of joy
together in store for us. I just have this one
last project here to finish up and then we will be
back together.
```

The project would start just hours later, and the world would come to know it as Desert Storm.

PART 9

The Storm

Desert Storm

Operation Desert Storm began in the early morning hours of January 17, 1991 with a coordinated series of air attacks by coalition forces made of fighter aircraft from Canada, France, Italy, Kuwait, Saudi Arabia, the United Kingdom, and the United States. Syph and Sweetness knew their first combat mission assignment two days before the war started and spent the preceding forty-eight hours in intensive mission planning. As the first combat mission for the squadron, they were required to brief the wing commander, Colonel Sandy Sharpe, about the tactics for the attack.

"Phillis" was the first name on the Panthers' flying schedule for day one of Desert Storm. He was leading Bianchi, a flight of four, which included Sweet as number two, Captain Gils Gilbert as number three, and First Lieutenant Jim Chambers as number four. Their briefing started at 0345 for a 0545 local takeoff.

The mission involved a coordinated four-ship attack of the ground-controlled intercept (GCI) integrated operations center (IOC) at Nukayb in western Iraq. Located near the Jordanian border and just north of Al Jouf, Saudi Arabia, the target area threat included anti-aircraft artillery (triple-A or AAA) up to 57mm, and man portable surface-to-air missiles (MANPADS).

It would be a long day. The plan was to launch from King Fahd, recover at Al Jouf to hot-pit refuel, then fly into Iraq for their combat mission, returning to Al Jouf to refuel, then flying back to King Fahd.

Ordnance for each A-10 included two G-model Imaging Infrared (IIR) Mavericks, six CBU-87 cluster bombs, a full load of 30mm combat mix, two AIM-9L heat-seeking air-to-air missiles, and an ALQ-131 ECM pod. Briefing complete, the pilots grabbed their life-support gear and personal weapons and headed out to the revetments protecting their jets. As each approached their Warthog, they felt a boost of confidence seeing all that firepower loaded. It was time to fight.

Fight's On

"Fight's on" are the words used on training missions to start a simulated attack, but they took on a whole new meaning on January 17. Bianchi flight took off on time and completed the first fuel stop as briefed. They departed Al Jouf northbound for the target area and, nearing the Iraqi border, "fenced in."

A fence check configures the aircraft for combat. Exterior lights are turned off, transponders are set to standby, emissions are reduced, combat systems are turned on, and self-protection measures are armed. The MASTER ARM switch is set to ARM, energizing the armament control system and arming the weapons for attack.

The attack began with Steve and Rob taking six-mile Maverick shots to predetermined locations within the target complex. It was Sweet's second live Maverick shot, and the thing leapt off his wing like a freight train in a huge cloud of white smoke. As he watched his Maverick race to the target, he noticed a series of faint flashes, which he first thought were glimpses of the sun, and soon recognized to be the muzzle flashes of AAA fire.

The flight continued to press their attack, which by all accounts was successful but not perfect. Steve's first Maverick shot missed, and Sweet missed one of the AAA targets with his CBU. One of the primary targets for this first mission were two large bunkers in the center of the compound. But when Bianchi flight showed up, these targets had already been hit the night before. Each had a hole on top, indicating penetration by a precision-guided bomb, probably the work of F-15Es.

The flight expended all of their weapons and scored hits on almost every piece of equipment in the target complex. Their mission had been to take out the eyes of the Iraqi military, and post-mission they were able to report leaving behind a blind spot near Nukayb. The flight returned to Al Jouf as briefed, then made the long flight back to King Fahd, landing both weary and relieved.

First Taste of Combat

The conduct of the first day's mission went as planned, and Steve remained very calm throughout. Sweet, however, was really fired up about this first combat mission and described himself as "unbelievably pumped up on adrenaline." The atmosphere in the squadron was that of Super Bowl game day, magnified by the prospect that the losing team had been destroyed.

The reality of combat operations started to take hold of the squadron as pilots returned with reports of being shot at. Everyone wanted to know what it was like. It was their first time on a two-way shooting range, and it was exciting. Each night, the pilots gathered and talked about the lessons they learned that day, mistakes they made, and educated everyone to avoid making those same mistakes. Steve wrote to Sharon about his experience.

January 18, 1991

The war is on. I flew four times yesterday. It
wasn't that bad. I now know what it is like to fly
with people shooting at you. Things went real well
yesterday. Sorry this is short, but I am up for
another four sorties today. The plan was a good
one and all the reports are great so far.

**A few days later, when he got a free moment, he provided
Sharon with more details.**

On the first day I led a 4-ship into Iraq. Nobody
engaged us until we got to the target. We found
our target and started to employ. As Rob Sweet
shot his Maverick missile I could see the flashes
from the small arms fire.

We later saw some airburst, but it was all underneath us. We were able to stay well above and they
really weren't effective. I felt like the cartoon
where the big guy with the long arms stiff arms
the little guy. The little guy keeps swinging, but
you can't reach him with short arms.

The sortie went very well. I was very proud of all
guys. The next target was unoccupied and we did
not get shot at. Guys are talking more about going
home. I think that may be a little premature.

Steve earned an Air Medal for his first mission, which read:

Captain Phillis displayed outstanding courage
and professionalism while leading a four-ship
of A-10 aircraft on an offensive counter air
mission against the Nukayb early warning/inter-
cept operations center in south central Iraq. In
the face of stiff anti-aircraft artillery fire
and shoulder fired surface-to-air missiles, the
flight succeeded in destroying three troposcatter

147

communications relay units, a RAT 3 phased array
radar, a Nanjing early warning radar, and flat
face, squat eye, Tiger 2D, tall king, spoon rest
and bar lock radars. The destruction of this key
element of Iraq's KARI command, control and communication system was vital to the establishment of
allied air supremacy. The professional skill and
airmanship displayed by Captain Phillis reflect
great credit upon himself and the United States
Air Force.

It would be the first of many awards he would earn during
Desert Storm. At the moment, however, he needed to ensure the
Panthers were adjusting well to combat flying.

Combat Flying

Now that everyone had seen combat, it was time to talk about
balancing mission and risk. Combat flying is about taking calculated risk. During the initial phases of Desert Storm, ground
troops remained in Saudi Arabia while the air campaign raged
on overhead. Early on, the coalition lost several aircraft executing low-altitude attacks. The losses caused leaders to rethink
their orders.

After the first several days, coalition air power leadership
announced changes to both daytime and nighttime employment
rules. Based on the premise that there was nothing worth dying
for on the ground during the air campaign, they restricted low-altitude flying and enacted several specific policies.

First, a ten-thousand-foot floor was established for weapons
employment for all aircraft, meaning that missiles and bombs had
to be released at an altitude that allowed the aircraft to recover
no lower than ten thousand feet. This directive kept coalition aircraft clear of most anti-aircraft artillery, the most prolific threat
to aircraft on the battlefield. While the hogs were prepared for
this order, several coalition partners were not.

Second, crews were instructed to leave areas of stiff enemy resistance in favor of finding less-defended targets whenever possible. Since there were plenty of targets to pick from in Kuwait and Iraq, it was pretty easy to do and made perfect sense.

Finally, reattacks were discouraged. A reattack means exactly that, attacking the same target a second time. The idea was that attacking a target brings immediate attention to the area, meaning suddenly everyone on the ground would be looking out for the attacking aircraft, increasing the likelihood of a counterattack. Put another way—shoot at a target and go find another target before they start shooting back.

Together, these tactics balanced the need for mission effectiveness with mission risk. Once the ground war started, everything changed. Now there would be something worth dying for down there, and the hogs would get down and dirty to support the guys on the ground. No altitude restrictions, no leaving just because the enemy was fighting back, and utilizing reattacks as required. But for now, discretion was the better part of valor.

This Is CNN

Anyone old enough to remember the first Gulf War watched it on CNN. While the invasion of Kuwait and buildup of Desert Shield were widely covered by a variety of news services, CNN came of age in Desert Storm. They were the only network reporting live from Baghdad on night one, and their unedited coverage brought modern warfare into everyone's living room.

Steve, his family, Sharon, Sweetness, Hendo, the Korean mafia, everyone at the Beach, Saddam Hussein, and anyone else with access to cable TV watched the war unfold in real time. Regular press briefings from Riyadh, Saudi Arabia gave the world an inside story, and provided images from camera-equipped high-tech weaponry employed against Iraqi targets.

The bright side was that the world learned about the pinpoint accuracy of precision-guided munitions and of the coalition's efforts to counteract Iraq's SCUD missiles, indiscriminate terror weapons of limited military value but great political value against coalition and Israeli targets. The coverage also had a dark side.

When the Iraqis filled a military bunker with civilians at nighttime, viewers saw the carnage of a precision strike up close and personal when an F-117 stealth fighter struck the target one evening. As terrible as that image was, the Panther pilots would see images that struck much closer to home.

Just days into the war, CNN began to broadcast images of abused coalition prisoners of war (POWs), and all of them were aviators. A British Tornado crew, along with U.S. Air Force, Navy, and Marine pilots were put on display for all the world to see.

The images were haunting, as most displayed visible signs of abuse, and those who spoke seemed under extreme duress. Every Panther pilot saw those battered faces and black eyes, as did everyone in their families. Though little was said about it, every pilot thought long and hard about the serious nature of the business they were in and rededicated themselves to winning, and winning fast.

CSAR Alert and Tasking

The images on CNN also injected new energy into the CSAR mission. Plans for Desert Storm included a robust search-and-rescue element, involving dedicated CSAR resources and elaborate plans for their use.

CSAR operations were managed at the Joint Rescue Coordination Center (JRCC) and involved coordination with AWACS, the alert A-10s at KKMC, and Special Operations Command Central (SOCCENT). Here's how it was supposed to work.

If someone got shot down, or saw an aircraft get shot down, the first call was to AWACS. On board was a controller trained and dedicated to the CSAR mission. The AWACS controller would verify the number, type, location, and status of the downed aircrew, and relay that information to the JRCC. In addition, AWACS would redirect aircraft to help protect the downed crew. The JRCC had direct communication with and scramble authority over the CSAR A-10s. If AWACS knew there was a survivor, or had reasonable suspicion of a survivor, CSAR hogs were launched to support any recovery operations.

JRCC also had a direct line to SOCCENT, who had CSAR helicopters and Special Operations forces on call for CSAR. SOCCENT forces would only be launched to rescue a known survivor who was in radio contact with friendly forces and within range of the rescue helicopters. In addition, SOCCENT forces would not be launched into areas of heavy enemy resistance, for fear of making the CSAR problem worse.

The hogs took the CSAR mission seriously, and they adopted the "Sandy" call sign to honor the heroic CSAR pilots from the Vietnam War who flew under that call sign. Steve and Rob sat CSAR alert during the last week of January, and this was really the first time that Sweet had the chance to sit down and talk to Steve about the war. It was also where Rob learned for the first time that Steve was engaged.

The Routine of War

Pilots are creatures of habit, so the start of combat flying allowed many to settle into a routine. Not that it wasn't dangerous, but after the newness of combat wore off, each pilot focused simply on their next mission and paid less attention to the overall air campaign. They also had to get used to another threat, which Steve described to Sharon a week into the war.

As you probably know by now Hussein fired off ten Scuds last night. They haven't been effective at all. They are a terror weapon only. The Patriots

```
[surface-to-air missiles used to intercept the
Iraqi Scuds] are doing a great job. It was scary
the first time I jumped into the bunker though.
The second time I fell asleep. They don't really
bother us that much now.
```

Steve and Rob also got into a combat routine, and Steve enjoyed flying with Rob. As a combat pair, Sweet flew twenty-eight of his first twenty-nine combat missions with Steve. As a result, they spent less time briefing the administrative portions of the mission and dedicated more time to weapons employment, target-area tactics, and threat study. Steve fell right into his usual calm, deliberate, and conservative approach to combat missions.

Because of the time and distances involved, each A-10 sortie involved about thirty minutes of actual fighting. The rest of the time was spent going and coming. The usual profile was to depart out of King Fahd with a full load of fuel and ordnance, in-flight refuel, then attack their first target. They would land at KKMC, rearm and refuel, fly a second mission, return to KKMC to rearm and refuel again, then fly their third mission and recover to King Fahd.

These typical three-go days left little time for planning and left pilots exhausted at day's end. But they were devastating Iraqi forces in Kuwait, although not yet to the point where they could not fight back. Steve shared his experience with Sharon.

```
I was up in Kuwait yesterday and yes one of the
oilfields was on fire. It was depressing but it
also strengthened my resolve. I guess he got a
couple airplanes up yesterday only to have them
all shot down. We own the skies.

The weather broke yesterday and we are back to
pounding on the enemy. Things are going well for
us again. We all hope that a ground war won't be
necessary but I think it is inevitable. Our army
```

is resting though right now while the Iraqi army
is going through a nightmare. Hopefully that will
make their job easier. We are into the second week
now and it is looking better for us. Once this is
over I am coming flying back to you.

Turning Up the Heat

The coalition air campaign was effective from the start, and as
successes mounted, our military leaders wanted to put even more
pressure on Iraq. At the end of January, General Glosson approved
a change allowing the A-10s to fly as low as four thousand feet
unless the enemy threat clearly dictated otherwise. This change
would increase both the A-10s' effectiveness and risk of getting
hit by enemy SAMs and AAA. It was the right call as far as the hog
pilots were concerned.

Getting the Warthogs lower would increase bombing accuracy
and allow them to use their favorite weapon, the 30mm gun. The
pilots welcomed the change, because coming home with a full gun
meant many targets went "unserviced." Since the stated goal was
to reduce the combat effectiveness of all Iraqi ground units to less
than 50 percent, coalition airpower needed to get after more targets with the same number of aircraft.

In response, the A-10s modified their target-area tactics. They
still started by first dropping their Mark 82 five-hundred-pound
bombs or CBU, then shooting Mavericks. But now they added
strafing as their final attack option before departing the target
area. Getting lower to use the gun increased combat effectiveness, but was not without risk.

Hog Down

During the first two weeks of Desert Storm, several A-10s were
struck by AAA and SAMs, yet each made it back to base. Every
time a wounded hog landed, it bolstered the confidence of every

A-10 pilot. Some pilots started to think that they could go the entire show without losing anybody. With each combat mission and passing day, confidence grew. All that came crashing back to reality, so to speak, on February 2.

Captain Dale "Storrman" Storr, an Alex A-10 pilot, was shot down that day by an SA-16 SAM. Storr had dropped his bombs and was strafing a truck park when he got hit. His wingman watched as the plane rolled over and called for him to eject, but he never saw a parachute. Dale ejected at low altitude, sailed through the fireball created when his jet impacted the ground, and landed at the feet of the Iraqis he'd just strafed.

Storr's wingman never saw him get out and never heard him on the radio. He went back and reported that Dale died in the crash. They went so far as to have a memorial service for him at King Fahd. Much to the surprise of many, Storrman was released by the Iraqis on March 6 after his capture and internment, but his initial status as "Killed in Action," or KIA, served as a wake-up call to many and reminded Steve that it was good to be a cautious pilot.

The Cautious Pilot

There are old pilots. There are bold pilots. There are few old, bold pilots. Steve was both an aggressive and cautious pilot. He was aggressive when he needed to be but remained a cautious guy who played it by the book. Sharon weighed in with her thoughts in no uncertain terms.

```
Steve, I love you and take care of yourself- Don't
be a hero, I won't be impressed by any medals! I
want you back in my arms so I can hug and pet you!
```

He was extremely disciplined in his combat weapons employment; such that, if he was unable to acquire the target or get a good Maverick lock, then he wouldn't shoot. He welcomed the change allowing for lower-altitude releases, but the problem with lower deliveries was that it put him in the heart of some SAM envelopes.

Based upon the rules, Steve and Rob did not use the gun all that much early in the war. By the time each had shot two Mavericks and delivered their six canisters of CBU, they had been hanging out in the target area long enough. Time over target, coupled with a directive to minimize exposure to ground fire, meant that the gun would be used sparingly, at least for now.

Tough Tasking

There were only two missions that Sweet remembers Steve being concerned about before takeoff. The first was flown on February 1 against an SA-6 "Gainful" SAM site. The SA-6 was a sophisticated Soviet-made surface-to-air missile that proved exceedingly lethal against the Israeli Air Force in the 1973 war. The Gainful remained a formidable threat to all coalition aircraft, especially the slow-moving A-10.

The mission was concerning not just because of the SA-6, but also because the system was being operated by Saddam's elite Republican Guards. Most Iraqi units in southern Kuwait were manned by poorly trained conscripts, but those in northern Kuwait and southern Iraq were better trained, equipped, and motivated.

As expected, resistance in the target area was much stronger and more effective than much of what Steve and Rob had seen so far. In the face of a more determined enemy, the Warthogs prevailed, but the glimpse into fighting against the Republican Guards was a reminder that the air war was far from over.

Steve earned another Air Medal on this mission, which read:

```
Captain Phillis demonstrated outstanding courage
and professional skill while performing suppres-
sion of enemy air defenses in Iraq-occupied
northern Kuwait. His outstanding calmness,
```

airmanship, and restraint under heavy enemy
anti-aircraft artillery fire resulted in the
destruction of three SA-6 transporter erector
launchers, a long track acquisition radar, and
a straight flush target tracking radar. Elimina-
tion of this deadly surface-to-air threat allowed
coalition forces to continue to prosecute the air
war against Iraqi Republican Guard forces in a
reduced threat environment and ultimately resulted
in saving many allied lives both in the air and on
the ground. The professional skills and airmanship
displayed by Captain Phillis reflect great credit
upon himself and the United States Air Force.

Pressing On

As February marched on, coalition air power continued pressing
their attacks while resistance put up by some Iraqi forces
increased. Steve tried to downplay the danger and told Sharon,
"Destroying an army that large takes time. Don't watch too much
CNN and rest assured that I will be back to love you forever." He
also wrote:

I flew two more combat sorties yesterday. Rob
Sweet does a real good job. I really enjoy flying
with him. I am getting more rest these days and
I still get nervous but not as bad. I don't get
cocky though and I am still being careful. After
all I have a wedding to go to. I am doing fine,
just hope this ends soon. We all want to go home.

Two days later, more news and thoughts from the desert.

The weather has held up well and we continue to
pound the enemy relentlessly. I can't imagine what
it is like for them. After all I had two good hot
meals yesterday and a good nights sleep and I know
they are not getting that.

It is hard to believe that Sadman thinks so little
of his people. Even still the enemy POWs all tell
the same story. I don't think the ground war will
take that much time. I just hope it starts soon so
we can all go home.

The Unwritten Rule

Almost a month into Desert Storm, Steve was number three in Thompson, a flight of four lead by Rick Shatzel. It was an early morning brief for a 0700 local time on target. As Steve was coming off target, Sweetness keyed the mike and called, "Thompson Three, break left!" Steve immediately responded with a max-performance turn while dispensing chaff and flares.

The SA-7 MANPAD shot at Steve bit on the flares and flew harmlessly by. Sweet's call and Steve's reaction avoided disaster. Key to this outcome was the mutual support provided between flight lead and wingman. Their contract was simple. While one was pressing an attack, the other was watching out for enemy fire. If the supporting fighter witnessed a SAM launch guiding on the attacking fighter, a SAM "break" call was made.

By this time in the war, Steve and Rob had seen a lot of AAA shot at them, and Steve had defeated several SAMs fired at him. While Sweet had not yet been shot at by a SAM, he'd called several SAM breaks for Steve. Once the missile was defeated, it was payback time.

The unwritten rule followed by most hog drivers was to immediately attack any unit that shot at them, especially SAM units. The idea was to teach the Iraqis that the penalty for shooting at coalition airplanes would be swift, immediate, and lethal retaliation. As a result, Sweet rolled in and shot a Maverick into the SAM site with good effects. Message delivered.

Keep Pressing

The pace of air operations continued to ramp up, and Steve reported.

> February 12, 1991
>
> I flew twice with Rob today. We were one and two in a four ship again. After takeoff we hit a tanker and topped off our fuel. We've then cruised out to the target. Overall the four ship went extremely well. I don't like flying in combat, but it is rewarding when you have a good mission.
>
> It sounds like he is suffering from mass defections. Hopefully he won't have much left when the army moves out.
>
> Our spirits are better lately. We are getting used to the threats. We are not being careless. But you now know how to deal with the threats. We also know how well the A-10 can really do. I guess a lot of it was fear of the unknown. Now we know what we are up against. We are all talking about not getting overconfident. No one can afford to get cocky.

Steve and Rob flew another two missions the following day, and Steve told Sharon, "Rob had an exceptional day. All in all, it was rewarding." After mailing off the letter, Steve was mindful that the following day was, in his words, the "day for lovers."

Happy Valentine's day

Steve was getting a lot of messages from home and sending some too. He arranged to have "gifts" delivered to Sharon on Valentine's Day. To quote his letter on the subject, "Let's just say that some of the things are for me and some are for you." He also wrote Sharon a Valentine's Day letter.

February 14, 1991

Happy Valentine's Day. It has been pretty quiet
today. You feel bad when you don't fly as you have
no idea how the war is going. Guys aren't bringing
back much ordnance today so they must be finding
good targets. I haven't heard the news recently so
I don't know what is happening. I heard that the
Iraqis are talking peace with the Soviets. It will
be interesting to see if anything develops for
that. I don't understand why they are subjecting
themselves to this.

I am not happy about delaying the ground war but
if it saves American lives it is the right decision. I just hope that they don't delay it too
long. We need to get this done and get back home.

I keep thinking about taxiing into Myrtle Beach
and seeing you there. Dropping off all my stuff
and running home with you. I really can't wait to
see you again. Like you I try to take it one day
at time. The hardest part is not seeing the end in
sight. But it is February 14, so not much left of
February. I still keep hoping to be home in March.
I want this to be over so I can get back to you.
It took me too long to find you and being separated from you is terrible.

After finishing his letter, Steve turned his attention to the next
day's tasking.

Tougher Tasking

The second mission that gave Steve pause for concern was the
tasking on February 15. Sweet could tell Steve was concerned
about their tasking. It was nothing specific that Steve said, but it
was a feeling that Sweet could undeniably sense. It was not fear.
It was justifiable concern.

The first major difference for this mission was that it was one hundred miles north of the Saudi/Kuwait border and further north than Syph and Sweetness had ever gone. Up until this point, most missions were flown within thirty miles of the border.

The second change was the routing into the target area. During most previous missions, the A-10s ingressed from out over the Persian Gulf. Their need to fly much further north for this mission required them to fly over Kuwait to and from the target area. This meant they would spend a lot more time over hostile territory.

Once they got to the target area, they would not be working alone. Unlike previous missions where they were sent against specific targets, their tasking was to a kill box being worked by a Forward Air Controller, or FAC.

The Kill Box

Airspace management and deconfliction were major challenges during Desert Storm due to the sheer number of aircraft flying in a relatively small space. After the war, more than a few pilots thought that the most dangerous flying they did was getting to and from the aerial refueling tracks. One way to efficiently manage airspace over a host of military targets was the kill box.

Kill boxes were thirty-mile-by-thirty-mile squares, divided into four quadrants, which allowed attacking aircraft more freedom of movement. A numbering system allowed pilots and FACs to seamlessly move to new target areas in response to changing conditions on the ground.

As the ground war approached, the A-10s were assigned to kill boxes and told to prioritize attacks first against artillery, then armor, then any other military target they could find. Kill boxes were often managed by either an A-10 "Nail" FAC or F-16 fast FAC. Steve and Rob were scheduled to work kill box AD8 with a fast FAC on February 15, tasked against the Republican Guards.

The Republican Guards

Steve and Rob began planning for the February 15 mission and spent extra time studying the Medina and Tawakalna Republican Guard Divisions. These units were far enough north that they had been spared many of the intense attacks endured by units closer to the Kuwait border. Intelligence briefers assessed these divisions at roughly 85 percent combat effective, much higher than units along the Saudi border.

Republican Guard units differed from others in several ways. First, they were better equipped, as their surface-to-air missile inventory included the SA-7, 14, and 16. In addition, these divisions operated the SA-13, an infrared/electro-optically guided missile mounted on a tracked vehicle, featuring a sophisticated guidance and control system designed to defeat western countermeasures. Each ten-thousand-soldier division was protected by two dozen SA-13 batteries arrayed in a space three miles wide by six miles long, which was a lot of concentrated firepower. Add in some 200 MANPADS and over 150 mobile AAA guns, and it made for a really dangerous place to employ the A-10.

These divisions were a lot more loyal to Saddam Hussein and thus more willing to fight. Steve and Rob expected to see more missiles and guns fired, and more of those missiles and guns would be guided. They again reviewed defensive reactions against SAMs, because the Republican Guards were both well-trained and had more experience from combat against Iran.

SAM defense was especially important, because at this point in the war, the Iraqis were not shooting at coalition aircraft all that often because they knew in return they would be immediately attacked. As a result, the Republican Guards limited their surface-to-air missile launches to situations where the gunners felt they had a higher probability of kill (Pk), or when the target aircraft had unwittingly flown into the heart of the operator's envelope. The result was that the Iraqis were taking shots with much higher Pk now a month into the war.

15 February 1991

Rick Shatzel knew the tasking for February 15 was difficult. As squadron commander, his job was to decide who flew each day, so he hand-picked the combat pairs for this mission. He would lead the first flight. Assistant Operations Officer Mike "Killer" Parsons would lead the second flight using the call sign "Pachmayr." Steve and Rob would fly later in the day, using the call signs "Enfield" 3-7 and 3-8. Before flying, Steve penned a quick letter to Sharon.

```
February 15, 1991

Hopefully we all will be going home soon. I think
it is getting closer to that day. Well sweetheart
I want to get this in the mail before I go fly. Rob
and I are going once. I miss you sweetheart. I love
you with all my heart and will love you forever.

Hope you had a happy Valentine's Day.

Love always, with all my heart.

Stephen
```

Syph and Sweetness were fragged (slang for assigned) for a 1400 local takeoff. They stepped from the Ops building into the bright light of the early afternoon. Each walked to a revetment where their hogs sat ready. Their combat load included two D-model TV Mavericks, CBU, a full load of combat mix in the gun, two AIM-9Ls, and an ECM pod.

During the preflight, Syph noticed artwork painted on the right side of the nose. It read, "The Last Crusade," and depicted the bullwhip used by Harrison Ford in the *Indiana Jones* movies. On his way up the ladder, Syph noticed that he was flying Hendo's jet. A good omen, he hoped.

Move to a Cooler Box

Enfield 3-7 flight departed King Fahd on time. The clear blue-sky day made the departure and pre-ingress air refueling easy. Rick's flight, already on its third combat mission of the day, Killer's flight, and Syph's two-ship were all sent to a kill box just south of Basra.

On the way, Shatzel's flight was diverted to attack a target near Bubian Island, just off the Kuwaiti coast. Parsons's flight was also reassigned to a new target, which left Enfield 3-7 alone for the kill box. As Syph checked in with the F-16 fast FAC, he could hear on the frequency that the area was hot.

He listened as flight after flight made SAM and AAA break calls. There was a ton of chatter on the frequency, and a lot of tense and intense radio calls. Steve evaluated the situation, and in compliance with the directives of his leadership, told the FAC that his two-ship would not be going up to that area because it was too hot. Steve repositioned the flight to kill box AF 7.

Steve moved his two-ship to the southern part of the kill box to look for targets in an area that was not quite so threatening. As the flight progressed South, he located a truck park that had previously been attacked. He noticed that there appeared to be some vehicles in the truck park still intact, so he dropped his CBU there. As he came off target, Killer's flight checked into the kill box.

Pachmayr 0-3: Enfield, Pachmayr.

Enfield 3-7: Go ahead.

Pachmayr 0-3: Roger, is your number two man, or are you just pullin' off a pass?"

Enfield 3-7: Pachmayr, I just came off the target, wingman's high, gettin' ready for a roll in.

Pachmayr 0-3: Roger, I have you both in sight. What we'd like to do is go to the west side of the hardball road. I see you're on the east side, and we'll drop our bombs on that battalion emplacement down here on the west side.

Enfield 3-7: That's fine. I'll keep my flight east. Be advised, when I was west of that road, I took some 23-millimeter air bursts, 10K.

After delivering CBU, Steve noticed a truck traveling southwest on the only road in the area, so he and Sweet followed the truck. Steve rolled in and strafed the truck but missed. The truck raced off the road and pulled into the center of a small circle of trucks parked on the south side of the road. Sweet rolled in and dropped his CBU on that truck park and covered about half the circle with bomblets. Steve called out that they had been in this target area long enough and directed the flight eastbound.

One More Pass

While flying eastbound, Steve spotted a lucrative target of riveted tanks in a three-mile-wide circle. He recalled numerous reports of decoy tanks. As a result, he spent a few minutes confirming that the tanks in the target area were real targets. There were no bomb craters anywhere in the formation, indicating that this unit had not come under recent attack in its present location.

At first, Steve wondered whether he should even attack these targets, fearing they were decoys. Getting late in the day, Steve rolled in and attempted to lock his TV Maverick onto one of the tanks. Unable to get a lock, he pulled off the target. Sweet rolled in behind his leader and also could not get a good TV Maverick lock. The flight was approaching bingo fuel, had delivered its CBU, and was unable to get Maverick locks. It was probably time to leave.

Instead, Steve repositioned the flight for what Sweet believed to be their final attack attempt. As Sweet approached the target in a climb to ten thousand feet, he rolled his A-10 on its side to do a belly check, a maneuver allowing him to see the area below him and to check and see if he was being shot at.

To his surprise, Sweet saw a SAM racing toward him, which had been launched from a riveted area in the center of the compound. The first thing he noticed was that the SAM was not moving on his canopy—meaning it was on a collision course with his airplane. Sweet saw the telltale smoke trail and red dot of the burning rocket motor closing fast.

Enfield 3-7: Chaff, flare! Chaff, flare!

Sweet deployed about half the flares in his airplane, and as the SAM closed in on his A-10, did a high-G roll to defeat the missile at end game.

Enfield 3-7: Okay, you got a missile just shot at you, it's over-
shot. Two, you're okay.

He had just survived the first SAM shot at him during the war but was not happy about the situation. At that moment, all communication discipline broke down. Sweet, his heart pumping and his body charged with adrenaline, shouted over the radio, "That son-of-a-bitch scared the shit out of me. Let's kill the fucker."

Steve rolled in on the revetment where the smoke-trail started and strafed, coming off target without seeing any secondary explosions. Secondaries were important because the rule of thumb for hog pilots was that if they didn't see anything blow up or catch on fire, they did not count it as a kill, even though post-war battle damage assessments would show many kills without any resulting fire or explosion.

Steve made a quick radio call to Killer.

Enfield 3-7: Pachmayr, Enfield had two SAM launches out of
this area, heads up.
Pachmayr 0-3: Roger, be advised that there was one taken a
hit, this morning, earlier.

Just a Bump

Rob watched Steve strafe the target, arcing around to the north, preparing for a reattack. Steve came off target in a climbing turn, then cleared his wingman in for the reattack. Sweet had no RWR indications and saw no SAMs, so he rolled in on the target. Without warning, he heard an explosion behind his airplane and felt a bump.

Not a violent bump, more like the bump he had felt previously when flying through another aircraft's jet wash. The bump had knocked the airplane from its turn to a wings-level position. At this moment, Steve called out, "there has been a missile launch" but the transmission was interrupted by Sweet's terse reply, "I know, I am hit, and I am heading south."

Sweet looked down the right side of his aircraft to assess the damage. Most of the right wing was gone. All that remained was twisted metal and fire burning the residual fuel and hydraulic fluid still left in the remnants of his right wing. Sweet quickly glanced inside and saw no indications of engine fire but saw the left-side hydraulic and left-side reservoir lights illuminated; a normal indication for the damage sustained.

Sweet reached over to isolate the hydraulic system to prevent loss of all hydraulics, trying to maintain aircraft control. He looked out again at his burning, battle-damaged airplane, which had just been hit by an SA-13. The warhead had worked as advertised, and shrapnel damage was draining the life out of his Warthog.

Not So Sweet

Sweetness was in a right-hand turn with a slight descent passing thirteen thousand feet when the SA-13 struck pay dirt, fulfilling the old fighter pilot adage, "It's the one you don't see that gets you." While Sweet's mortally wounded Warthog rolled out of control, Steve called and said, "try and roll your wings level," to which Sweet replied, "I can't. I can't."

The stick in Sweet's hand went to mush, and now the airplane was pointing straight down. Rob looked through the HUD and saw a face full of sand and, plummeting through sixty-five hundred feet, called to Steve, "I'm out, I'm out," and pulled the ejection handles with much more than the forty-five pounds of pull required for seat activation.

In half a second, the canopy was gone and his seat headed up the rails. The rocket motor fired, and two seconds later his chute opened. Sweet heard the whoosh of the canopy separating and felt the jerk of parachute-opening shock. He immediately discarded his mask and watched his once-mighty hog spiral to the desert floor below, trailing white smoke. It hit the ground with such a force that the wreckage looked like a grease smear.

Rob now had a five-minute parachute ride to the desert below and time to think about the fact that he was descending into the middle of the unit that he and Steve had just finished bombing. He saw muzzle flashes from the ground and heard bullets whizzing by his head.

CSAR Mode

Steve watched as the ground below erupted in a hail of anti-aircraft fire, some of which was surely aimed at Sweetness. He instinctively switched to combat search and rescue mode. At first, he watched helplessly as Sweet ejected, then got to work, noting a good chute. The green, tan, white, and orange panels of the C-9 canopy made it easier for him to keep sight of during the descent. He reached over to the INS control display unit and hit the MRK push-button, storing the ejection site coordinates. Now it was time to talk.

Steve reached over and switched his UHF radio to the AWACS frequency to alert Bulldog of the shootdown, which immediately set search and rescue forces in motion. He then called for additional firepower. If Sweet were to land in an area far enough away from the Medina Division they had just finished bombing, Steve was going to do everything he could to protect his wingman until the CSAR forces could launch a rescue mission.

It was time to go. Sweetness had safely ejected, his last known position had now been relayed to AWACS, and help was on the way. Steve had ample opportunity to leave, and plenty of reasons to depart, now low on fuel and weapons.

The thought of leaving never crossed his mind. Not for a second. His sense of responsibility as a flight lead, flight commander, weapons officer, and American airman would not allow it. It was time to get back to work.

Bagged

Keeping sight of Sweetness under canopy was a top priority, so Steve advanced both throttles to MAX and continued a climbing left-hand orbit. Smoke and dust from their recent attacks now mixed with the smoke of small arms, AAA, and SAM firings. The ground below literally erupted, and it was all fixed on the Silent Gun still orbiting directly above.

After alerting AWACS, call sign Bulldog, Steve switched back to the kill box frequency to talk to Pachmayr. Getting more aircraft overhead right now was critical. His attention was divided between the radio, keeping sight of Sweetness, and aimed fire from below. He looked down at his lineup card and found the pre-briefed code word for friendly aircraft down, then keyed the mike.

Enfield 3-7: Pachmayr, Enfield 3-7.

Pachmayr 0-3: Roger Enfield, understand you're departing?

Enfield 3-7: Negative, I need you to come over and CAP my position.

Pachmayr 0-3: Roger, I'm on my way. I'll be there in about four minutes.

Pachmayr 0-3: Pachmayr's approaching the hardball roads, say position.

Enfield 3-7: Okay, we got two SAM launches. My wingman is bag at this time. I have him in sight. I'm just about to the topper point [Bingo fuel, meaning almost out of fuel]. I want you to come over to my position, do you have me in sight?

Pachmayr 0-3: Negative. I'm approaching the hardball inter-section from the north. What's your position from the big hardball intersection?

Enfield 3-7: I'm not sure which one you're talkin' about. You see this big smoke cloud down here to the east of your target?

Pachmayr 0-3: Affirmative, I see several smoke clouds down here. If you take the target area we hit and go straight down to the south, there's a hardball-road intersection. Two-hardball-road intersection, like an X.

Enfield 3-7: Yeah, come south from that intersection. Do you see a big dust cloud over here?

Pachmayr 0-3: I see two white smokes on the ground. Looks like from a Nail FAC. Can you see those?

Enfield 3-7: Negative, I don't.

Pachmayr 0-3: Can you pop a flare?

Enfield 3-7: Popping one.

Pachmayr 0-3: Partner, I still don't have your flare in sight. I'm gonna pop one now.... Do you have a flare in sight?

The Light Show

Popping high-visibility pyrotechnic flares to help Killer locate his position was the right thing to do but came at a great cost. As the lone aircraft circling over ten thousand enemy soldiers, highlighting his A-10 made him a target for every Iraqi SAM and AAA operator in the division. It was a risk Steve willingly took without any regard for his personal safety.

Then it happened. Steve felt a shudder in the flight controls and a thump from behind. He quickly turned around to see smoke and fire. He saw twisted metal from the left engine nacelle flailing in the slipstream. Small holes peppered the right engine nacelle, aft fuselage, and both tails.

Inside the cockpit, he saw a light show, including MASTER CAUTION, FIRE (L ENG) PULL, L ENG OIL PRESS, L HYD PRESS, L HYD RES, L FUEL PRESS, L GEN, PITCH SAS, YAW SAS, ANTI SKID, and BLEED AIR LEAK. He reset the MASTER CAUTION and quickly concluded that these lights were consistent with the damage he saw, and he knew at that moment it was time to go.

He turned Hendo's wounded A-10 to the southwest and put KKMC, the nearest divert field, on the nose. He retarded the left engine throttle to see if he could extinguish the fire, which prevented him from climbing any higher. The aircraft was now trailing black smoke, and the BLEED AIR LEAK light was getting his attention since it meant that four-hundred-plus-degree air was now circulating unsupervised in areas not designed for such heat. At that moment, things went from bad to worse.

MASTER CAUTION, FIRE (R ENG) PULL, and another light show indicated a right engine fire. With total hydraulic failure pending, he reached down to his left and selected MAN REVERSION to properly place the flight controls to manual reversion. He again looked over his shoulder and confirmed that both engines were now on fire. He pushed the left throttle to MAX and picked up speed. More heat out the back end meant more thrust, and he needed to get as much distance as possible between him and the Iraqi army.

As the fires burned, Steve knew his Warthog would not make it all the way to KKMC, and he returned to the radio, still thinking about his responsibility to others.

Enfield 3-7: Pachmayr, Enfield.
Pachmayr 0-3: Enfield, Pachmayr. Go.
Enfield 3-7: Yeah, recommend you egress.

The fires showed no sign of letting up, and in fact intensified. A full three minutes and forty-five seconds after Sweetness ejected, an eternity for a single fighter aircraft over an intensely hostile enemy division, Steve keyed the mike. In a voice as calm and cool as ever, without a trace of fear or worry, he made his last radio call of the day.

Enfield 3-7: Pachmayr, Enfield 3-7 is bag as well.

The Flagpole

Six thousand eight hundred and twenty-one miles away, for reasons still not explained to this day, the flagpole in front of the Phillis family house in Rock Island simply snapped in two.

PART 10

The Search

Frantic Search

Killer knew he was close to Syph's location and was searching high and low for any sign of him. His search was complicated by all the smoke of bombs going off and SAM firings, and dust from explosions and AAA batteries. Without a radar, it would be really tough sledding. Then his wingman, Dave "Smiley" Hanaway, piped in with a good idea.

> Pachmayr 0-4: Request to go to AWACS freq.
> Pachmayr 0-3: Roger, you're cleared to go to AWACS freq.
> at this time. Keep me informed on Fox [FM inter flight radio].

Smiley knew the first order of business was to get AWACS to find Pachmayr's current position, so he got right on it.

> Pachmayr 0-4: Bulldog, Bulldog, Pachmayr 0-3.
> Bulldog: Pachmayr, go ahead.
> Pachmayr 0-4: Roger, do you have my position?
> Bulldog: Negative, Pachmayr, say mission number please.

Pachmayr 0-4: Roger, 5003 Charlie. Let me give you an Alpha
point. We're close to Alpha 0-9.
Bulldog: Pachmayr, Bulldog, searching for your position.

Smiley waited for a moment, then listened impatiently as
Bulldog talked to other aircraft. He knew time was precious and
was getting agitated, so he keyed the mike and said, with some
authority:

Pachmayr 0-4: Bulldog, get my position now!

Bulldog got the message.

Bulldog: Copy Pachmayr, searching right now.

Efforts by AWACS to locate Pachmayr amidst the hundreds of
aircraft flying over Kuwait were hampered in part by equipment
settings. The A-10's ejection seat contained a Survivor Locator
Beacon, and radio device that AWACS could track upon activation. During peacetime operations, the beacon was set to AUTO,
meaning it would start transmitting immediately upon ejection.
When the Warthogs were reconfigured for combat, the
beacon was switched to MANUAL, disabling the automatic
function and requiring the pilot to manually activate the beacon.
This action prevented enemy forces from using the beacon as a
homing device, but also prevented friendly forces from quickly
identifying the locations of downed pilots. Smiley would just
have to wait.
While waiting for an affirmative response from Bulldog,
Smiley got a call from another flight wanting to help.

Buckshot 0-1: Pachmayr, Buckshot. Can we help you?
Bulldog: Pachmayr, Bulldog. Do you have an emergency?
Pachmayr 0-4: We have two A-10s that are bag at this time,
stand by.
Bulldog: Copy.

Buckshot 0-2 was flying in formation with his leader and caught sight of two A-10s below them.

Buckshot 0-2: Two, I have him in sight. You got him at your
　　left eleven o'clock, low, for two miles.
Buckshot 0-1: Okay, left eleven o'clock, low?
Buckshot 0-2: Yeah, left eleven o'clock, low, two miles.
Buckshot 0-1: Okay, we'll find him. Help me, vector me
　　on him.
Buckshot 0-2: Come hard left, look down at your left eleven.
Buckshot 0-1: Okay, I've got an aircraft.
Buckshot 0-2: Enfield two, one.
Buckshot 0-1: These guys are employing. That's not Enfield.
Buckshot 0-2: Okay.

Hopes dashed, Smiley continued to press Bulldog.

Pachmayr 0-4: Bulldog, Pachmayr. How you comin'?
Bulldog: I've got you. Positive contact. What's the problem?
Pachmayr 0-4: Roger, we have two A-10s that are bag at this
　　time. We're searching for them visually, and stand by.

There is an old adage that no good deed goes unpunished. While Smiley was talking to AWACS and watching his flight lead search for Syph, he spotted a SAM launch. The SAM appeared to be guiding on Killer.

Pachmayr 0-4: One, break left! . . . get some junk comin'
　　out! [chaff and flares]
Pachmayr 0-3: Say again.
Pachmayr 0-4: Get some junk comin' out! . . . Egress south.
　　Go 1-8-0.... We're taking some SAM launches from back
　　there at the road intersection...head 1-8-0.

Killer hammered down with his left ring and pointer finger to get chaff and flares out, yanked hard on the stick, and watched the missile fly on by. He didn't see where it came from, and asked Smiley if he knew more.

> Pachmayr 0-4: I couldn't see where it really came from. I kinda saw the smoke trail. I'm at your left eight, there... we're okay now.

Crisis averted, they got back to work searching for Syph and Sweetness.

The Fog of War

A lot of things were happening at once. People were running up and down the crowded isles of the AWACS trying to figure out who was talking to who. Pilots were hearing bits and pieces of information. Some radio calls were missed, others misunderstood. While there is no doubt that everybody was trying to do the right thing and help, they just couldn't break through the fog of war.

> Pachmayr 0-4: Bulldog, Pachmayr.
> Bulldog: Go ahead, Pachmayr.
> Pachmayr 0-4: Are you talking to any Enfields? Are you painting any of them?
> Bulldog: Enfield is up in the area, affirmative.
> Pachmayr 0-4: Okay, you got two paints on them?
> Bulldog: Standby, we're talking to them on Red 2. What do you need?
> Pachmayr 0-4: Okay, understand you're talking to both of them?
> Bulldog: Copy, stand by one.
> Pachmayr 0-4: Okay one, two. Recommend egress. Bulldog is talking to both Enfields.... They're heading 1-8-0.
> Pachmayr 0-3: Roger. We're heading 1-8-0.
> Bulldog: Pachmayr, Bulldog, we are talking to Enfields, go ahead.

Pachmayr 0-4: Okay, that's just what we wanted to check on
'cause we understood they were bag.

Bulldog: Stand by, we're talking to them now. We'll find out.

Pachmayr 0-4: Can you give us vectors to them?

Bulldog: Stand by, we'll get that.

Pachmayr 0-4: Bulldog is gonna vector us to them in a second.

Pachmayr 0-3: Bulldog, Pachmayr 0-3.

Bulldog: Go, Pachmayr 0-3.

Pachmayr 0-3: I'm back up on your freq. with my wingman,
now. Gimme a vector to Enfield if you got him in sight.

Bulldog: Alright, Enfield...wait, stand by one.

Pachmayr 0-3: Bulldog, break, break, Pachmayr 0-3, give me
a vector to Enfield.

Bulldog: We're searching for them right now, sir, we're radio
contact...break, break, Enfield 3-7, are you up on this
frequency?

Pachmayr 0-3: Standby this frequency, please. Enfield,
Enfield, Pachmayr 0-3 on victor [VHF radio used inter
flight].

Pachmayr 0-3: Enfield, Enfield, Pachmayr 0-3, victor.

Bulldog: [Talking to Pachmayr 0-3] Were you radio with
Enfield, and did you see him?

Pachmayr 0-3: The problem was we never did see him. He
called for us to some and give him some CAP. I cannot
get him on any radio at this time. There is a lot of talking
going on the radio and I can't get through to him.

Bulldog: Understand. We're no radios with him either,
standby for his last posit [position].

Pachmayr 0-3: Roger.

Despite this setback, nobody was ready to give up just yet.
Steve's last series of radio calls convinced Killer and Smiley that
they had two survivors to look for.

Unanswered Calls

Bulldog and Pachmayr tried to reach Enfield on every normal frequency they had, but no response. Running low on fuel, Pachmayr made one final attempt to raise Syph on the radio. Killer switched his UHF radio frequency 243.0, known as Guard, the international distress frequency monitored by all military pilots. It was an open frequency, meaning it could be monitored by anyone, including the Iraqis. It was the frequency of last resort for use in emergency situations only, and this certainly qualified.

Pachmayr 0-3: Enfield, Enfield, Pachmayr 0-3 on Guard, how do you read me?

No response.

Pachmayr 0-3: Enfield, Pachmayr 0-3 on Guard, how do you read?

Again, no response.

Pachmayr 0-3: Bulldog, unsuccessful link-up with Enfield 3-7 for Pachmayr 0-3. Are you reading him at all?
Bulldog: Just did a check on Guard with him...standby for his last posit [position].
Pachmayr 0-3: Roger, copy.
Bulldog: Break, break, Pachmayr 0-3, Bulldog.
Pachmayr 0-3: Bulldog, Pachmayr 0-3. Go.
Bulldog: Yeah, coordinates for his last posit unable at this time.

Unable to see, hear, or find Syph, it was time for Pachmayr to go, at least for the moment.

Pachmayr 0-3: Roger, can you get me a tanker so I can come back in here. I'm getting low on gas.

Killer was determined to return and continue looking for Syph, without knowing that reinforcements were already on the way.

CSAR Scramble

A lot of guys flew through a lot of bullets looking for Syph and Sweetness, starting with Killer and Smiley, and followed shortly thereafter by the CSAR guys. Joe "Root" Rutkowski was sitting CSAR alert as Sandy 1, along with Greg "Guru" Mooneyham as Sandy 2. It was Friday afternoon and time for the CSAR crew to swap out, so Root and Guru were headed out the door to their hogs to crank up, take off, and patrol the border for about twenty minutes until the new Sandy flight was on station, then head back to King Fahd.

They got a call to "go ahead and crank, but don't go anywhere." AWACS had just notified the JRCC that two A-10s had been shot down. Root and Guru were scrambled, and JRCC tasked the recovery to SOCCENT. SOCCENT immediately began planning a mission, but with no voice contact, a location one hundred miles north of the border, and stiff enemy resistance, a rescue mission would not be launched straight away. The Sandys needed to find at least one survivor first.

Once airborne, the Sandys were told that one A-10 had been shot down and the other was missing. As they neared the search area, they found out both were missing and assumed shot down just north of Kuwait. They arrived overhead of Enfields' last known position and got straight to work.

Root's job was to drop down and find a survivor on the ground while Guru held high, watching out for threats and covering Root while coordinating search and rescue forces with AWACS. It was getting late in the day, so time was running short. Step one was to find Sweetness or Syph.

Root and Guru knew that the Republican Guard forces arrayed below had shot down a couple of airplanes, and by the looks of things, they wanted a couple more. The Sandys were working hard just to keep themselves safe as Root kept calling and calling and calling out for "Enfield" on the radio.

As darkness fell without any response, Root and Guru could now clearly see just how many guns and missiles were being shot at them. It was scary. They kept looking and calling but no luck. Determined to find Syph and Sweetness, they refused to leave and were getting low on fuel—very low, actually, much lower than they should have.

Guru and Root agreed they needed to get out and get gas, and that there wasn't much else they could do. They started heading south and realized they were really, really low on fuel. Guru called the AWACS and said, "We need a tanker, or else we're not even going to get home."

AWACS coordinated with a KC-135 who radioed them directly and said, "Meet us at a certain point on the map." Guru said, "Okay," and when he found the point on his map noticed it was well inside Iraq. He thought, "This [unarmed] KC-135 is going to meet us in Iraq? These guys are ballsy." They took just enough gas to make it back King Fahd, then headed back to share everything they knew about Enfield.

After landing, Root walked up to Guru and said, "I probably feel worse than you look right now." They were exhausted from the search, being shot at for hours, and kind of scared. Guru looked at Root and said, "You know, as bad as I feel, there's a couple of guys on the ground that feel a whole lot worse right now."

Down on the Ground

Rob was feeling a whole lot worse at this point. He had landed fifty yards from an Iraqi T-72 tank, right in the middle of the unit he and Steve had just bombed. Hordes of soldiers descended upon him and stripped off his flying gear while beating him with hands, fists, and rifle butts. After a half-dozen blows to the head, he prayed, "God, don't hit me again." Finally, a group of Iraqi officers pulled him away, threw him in the jeep, and raced him into a nearby bunker.

In the ensuing days, he would be driven to Baghdad blindfolded and tied up with ropes. When he arrived, they shoved him into a small room and beat him with a thick rubber hose, careful not to break any bones. The beatings began a regular pattern of torture and interrogations Rob would endure through the end of the war. He was kicked, punched, slapped so hard his eardrum burst, and he was repeatedly questioned with a gun pressed against his temple. It was the stuff of nightmares.

He, along with all the other Panther pilots, had been warned to expect poor treatment at the hands of the Iraqis. Rob whispered a lot of prayers, quietly sang his favorite songs, and labored over the thought of his mother crying at the news that her son was a prisoner of war. He took comfort in the fact that his country would do everything possible to secure his safe return, especially his fellow hog drivers.

Missing Panthers

Hendo was flying back to King Fahd after sitting CSAR alert at KKMC when he heard AWACS trying to raise an "Enfield" call sign on the radio. He didn't think much of it, assuming that it was just someone who was not up on the right frequency. He landed and returned to an empty room, which got his attention but not especially so. There were a million reasons why Steve would not be there at that time. As time passed, Hendo started thinking that maybe there was more to it than that.

Word filtered back to the Panthers that two of their A-10s had been shot down. There was a scramble to piece together bits of information and conflicting reports. By late afternoon, the word was out—Syph and Sweetness had been shot down. The feeling of shock and disbelief spread through the squadron. Speculation started.

Syph's radio calls immediately following Sweetness's ejection supported the conclusion that Sweetness had successfully ejected, but there was no word as to whether he had survived the ejection or landing. Steve's fate was even less certain. What was clear to the Panthers was that Syph's last radio call was undeniable evidence his aircraft had been seriously damaged beyond the point of being flyable. With no other eyewitnesses, his fate would remain a mystery.

The pilots were summoned by their squadron commander, Rick Shatzel, who told the pilots that Steve and Rob had not returned from the afternoon go. It was a short meeting, and the pilots returned to their rooms. Steve's roommates were asked whether they wanted to fly the next day, and each answered yes. And then the wondering began.

Calling to Say Hello

One of the downsides of CNN's round-the-clock coverage was the near-immediate reporting of friendly losses. As soon as word got out that an A-10 was shot down, the phone lines at Alex and Myrtle Beach went crazy. Desperate wives and loved ones flooded the base with hysterical calls, and Sharon described the scene in an interview years later.

> *Saturday when they announced that an A-10 went down, a lot of people panicked. I got a call from Christy at twelve noon to tell me that it was no one from Myrtle Beach, then I called everyone—your mom and dad, my mom and dad, Jeanie, Tamara, Vicki, Emily, to tell them. Some of the phone lines were out and they couldn't get a hold of Linda Dunn, so I drove over to tell her. Boy was she happy to see me.*

The problem was compounded by a lack of connectivity. Desert Storm predated the internet and personal cell phones. King Fahd was limited to a small bank of phones that only made outgoing calls, so Panther pilots had few opportunities to call home. The problem was that when they did call home, they got an earful from well-meaning family members complaining, "I was worried sick when I heard on CNN that an A-10 got shot down."

The rules were crystal clear that pilots could not talk about what they were doing or what anyone else was doing. The solution some devised was to strategically call home to say, "Hey, just calling to let you know I'm alright." Sandy Sharpe got wind of these calls and blew a stack. "There will be no calls—you insensitive bastards. You want to make your family feel good? You don't realize what you're doing to everyone else's families!"

The problem of course was that many of the pilots could not immediately call home. Some were flying, others sitting alert, and others busy planning or debriefing. In the end, the rules were clear to every pilot. Nobody calls home until the official notification process had run its course. No exceptions.

Knock It Off

In addition to losing two Warthogs on February 15, several others were damaged, including one flown by the Alex wing commander Colonel Dave Sawyer. The losses were reported up the chain of command, as required. After General Glosson gathered the details, he went to talk to his boss, Lieutenant General Chuck Horner, commander of U.S. and allied air operations.

General Horner had flown over one hundred missions in Vietnam, earning the Silver Star as an F-105 Wild Weasel pilot. He spent his entire career in fighter aviation and had command experience at every level. He also had a son who flew A-10s in the United States Air Force, a fact known by most Panthers.

After careful consideration, he made the best military decision in support of the air campaign, personal feelings aside. General Horner decided to restrict A-10 operations to targets closer to the border, adding, "You're not going that far north anymore." Additionally, he directed that Warthogs had to stay above ten thousand feet and not use the gun. It was the right call but a tough pill for the Panthers to swallow.

In fact, the Panthers thought it sucked. Danno Swift was pretty vocal about it. "It was a Republican Guards unit. Let's go kick some ass!" He continued, "Bullshit. Let's take the whole fuckin' armada up there tomorrow. B-52s, F-15Es, F-111s, and two hundred forty high-order detonations."

He reminded everyone about the work they had done the week before against another Republican Guard unit, the Tawakalna Division, which was packed into a formation six miles long and three miles wide. They took four separate eight-ships across the target in an hour. They divided the division so each flight had a quarter. Within three minutes, they had forty-eight high-explosive bombs going off and not a whole lot of return fire.

But orders were orders, so the pilots reluctantly fell in line. After breaking up for the night, many went back to the hooch to think about what was going on back home.

Notification

It was Friday night in Rock Island, Illinois when Diane Phillis answered the knock at the front door of the family's home. Standing before her was an Air Force officer assigned to the nearby base with the unenviable task of telling this mother of five that her oldest son was now missing in action.

The family quickly gathered and shared the news. The officer asked everybody in the family not to say anything, because it might hamper search and rescue efforts, so the family sat, in silence, and waited. A similar scene played out at the home of Rob Sweet's parents.

Sharon got home from a great day at work and admired the dozen red roses, among other things, that Steve sent her for Valentine's Day. She had plans to go out but decided instead to stay in for the evening.

At about seven o'clock there was a knock at the door, and four
Air Force members in dress blue uniforms stood somberly outside. Sharon was new to the Air Force way of life but knew what it
meant when blue uniforms showed up during a war.

She didn't recognize any of them, even though two of them,
Chip and Peggy Toldy, lived down the street and regularly came to
the house to check on Sharon at Steve's request. She invited them
in, but it was as all a blur. She had not been watching CNN, so she
had heard nothing about A-10s getting shot down, but she understood Steve was missing in action. Colonel Dallager, the wing
commander, asked her not to discuss the news with anyone, again
to protect search and rescue work underway.

Sharon was handed a hastily typed letter, like the one delivered
to Bud and Diane Phillis, which she set down without reading.
Later that evening, alone and unable to sleep, she picked it up.

15 February 1991

Dear Ms Taflan

On behalf of the Chief of Staff, United States Air
Force, I regret to inform you that Stephen Phillis'
jet was reported missing approximately 8:30 a.m.,
eastern standard time, February 15, 1991 over the
Northwest part of Kuwait. All the allied countries
began a search immediately; however, at this time
we have no further information on Stephen's condition or whereabouts. Please be assured we're doing
everything we can to determine his condition, and
we'll let you know as soon as we can.

Again, on behalf of the Chief of Staff, please
understand our thoughts and prayers are with you
and Stephen's family.

Sincerely
JOHN R. DALLAGER, Colonel, USAF
Commander

Word of the shootdowns spread quickly through the A-10 community, and reactions were mixed. Shock, disbelief, denial, and anger topped the list. People who knew Syph best were certain he would be found, their only question was how long they would have to wait.

In true Weapons School fashion, when Steve's FWIC instructor heard the news, he filled out a Close Air Support ride grade sheet and marked "unsatisfactory" for defensive reaction. He decided not to send it, but if he had, Steve would have laughed out loud when he read it. Back at Myrtle Beach, there was not a lot of laughter to be heard.

Night Under the Stars

The Panthers rallied around Sharon. People brought over food, offered to sit with her, and stepped up to do anything she needed. Nothing helped, but she was thankful for the efforts. She was not in the mood to talk and had trouble sleeping.

The next day, at about three o'clock in the morning, Sharon went for a walk by the lake. She sat down, looked up at the stars, and started talking to Steve. She kept looking up while talking to him, then asked "why am I looking up to talk to you? I should be looking out to the east or west, but I keep looking up, and I don't like it. You better not be up there!"

Sharon was the strong one. Others came to cry on her shoulder. On the outside she was strong, but on the inside she was lost. She wouldn't eat, and she refused to think he was dead. For once, she followed orders and refused to talk to anyone other than her parents, the Phillis family, and her new Air Force family. She did not want to give the Iraqis anything they could use against Steve if he were a POW.

The Phillis family took a similar approach. They would not speak to the media and waited like everyone else for news about

Steve. While Sharon and the Phillis family waited patiently, support began pouring in from every direction.

Support Pours In

While support for Sharon came in the form of visitors, support for Bud and Diane came from visitors and letters.

Dear Bud and Diane,

At the time of this letter, we have still not heard anything regarding Steve's status other than MIA. That very term, MIA, seems like something from the past. Now it hits home. Daily we get letters with clippings about Steve from friends all over the country. They know of our concern and feelings without asking. Often the letters just contains clippings, the sender, like me, not knowing what to say.

I guess I have nothing to add except our personal sense of loss and daily tears with the lack of news. You must know of our feelings, and you must translate that into the proper intensity of our emotion.

We have no platitudes. I can only guess how you feel. But, I think I know how I would feel if I were to be the victim. And that would probably be the same way you feel if it were you and not Steve.

Yet Steve was/is a warrior, but his choice. Recognized as the best of the best. Few of us are that good in our vocation. Steve's greatest pride probably was his recognition of your love and admiration of his attainments as a man.

We will continue our add our voices to the prayers of the community.

Most people did not know what to do or say, and who could blame them? Steve's Air Force family back at the Beach kept in close contact with Sharon and the Phillis family, offering support in every way imaginable. At times it was a bit overwhelming, but nobody was able to provide the one thing they all really needed—news about Steve.

The Wait

Despite all efforts to find Steve, nothing worked. All those pilots flying through all those bullets came back empty. Nothing was heard in response to all the radio calls made. Mission debriefs painted a rough picture of what happened but provided no definite answers.

Desert Storm marched on, and the pace of flight operations intensified. As the ground war approached, the gloves were coming off. The A-10s would be tasked to provide close air support to coalition troops in close combat with the enemy. Lives would be on the line. General Glosson made his position clear in a message to every American pilot.

> All of you heard me say earlier that not one thing in Iraq is worth dying for, and that was true. Sometime in the next week, there is going to be a lot worth dying for in Iraq. We call them American soldiers and marines. When I said that I wanted a minimum loss of life, we cannot draw distinctions between Americans who die. If a marine dies or a soldier dies, it's all the same to me as one of you dying. For that reason, there will be no restrictions placed on you by anyone. The individual fighter pilot or flight lead will decide what is necessary.

The Panthers and their fellow coalition pilots took this message to heart at the start of the ground war. The hogs were down at low altitude, and there were plenty of stories told of A-10s down at a hundred feet, and lower, putting warheads on foreheads. Countless lives were saved by their heroics.

On February 28, 1991, offensive air operations against the Iraqi military were suspended. One hundred hours after the initiation of offensive ground combat operations, the fighting was over. For the Panthers, however, the war was not over. The elation and relief felt by everyone was tempered by the sadness and uncertainty of the fate of their missing comrades.

In the days leading up to the signing of the cease-fire and subsequent POW release, all eyes at King Fahd and Myrtle Beach were fixed on CNN. Interviews with captured Iraqis after the war claimed they saw two parachutes and shot down two planes the day Syph and Sweetness went missing. Everyone hoped that Steve was still alive and just missing, but the agony of not knowing kept mounting.

Homecoming

In early March, word came down to the squadron that POWs were soon to be released. Each POW was assigned an escort officer, a friend from the squadron whose job it would be to meet him immediately following his release from captivity. Rick Shatzel selected Bull Chambers as Rob Sweet's escort officer, and much to Hendo's dismay, Gils Gilbert to escort Steve.

Hendo desperately wanted to be part of the liberation of his friend. He went back to the room and grabbed a handful of things he knew Steve would want immediately. Nine letters from Sharon, half a pack of Marlboro lights, a can of Copenhagen, five Havana cigars, a samurai scarf from Korea, and a few photographs. He quickly stuffed the items into a plastic bag and included this note:

```
Syph, well what can I say that won't sound trivial
and trite. It's great to have y'all back! I wish
I could have been there to meet you but Shatzel
wanted someone from the flight. Not only do I
```

```
have to pack all your shit, but you take away my
best drinking buddy! Gils and I packed up what we
thought you would need, but I am throwing a few
extras in this bag. Sha Sha is doing well as I
hope you know by now. What else can I say? Words
don't describe it, buddy. Greg.
```

He stuffed the note into the plastic bag and delivered it to Gils, who was then off to the airport.

On March 6, some prayers were answered as coalition prisoners of war were released. It was a moment of indescribable anticipation as the world watched these newly liberated men and women walk free. For many family and friends, the POW release was the first piece of information concerning their loved ones since they were listed as missing in action.

Sharon was at work and wasn't watching TV when the news coverage started. The sight of Rob Sweet walking off the plane brought an incredible sense of relief to his family and a big boost to the Phillis clan. But hope was crushed as the last POW deplaned. No Steve. It was the lowest moment the Phillis family had ever known. The agony continued.

Earlier that day, Sharon got a phone call from a well-intentioned friend letting her know the Panthers were preparing for the release of two POWs, which would have been Rob and Steve. Later that day she got another call, letting her know that the release of two POWs had not been confirmed. The caller didn't want Sharon's feelings hurt if something else should happen.

At last she got a call at work to tell her Steve was not a POW. She drove home, went into the house, sat down by herself, and wondered, "Well, he's not a POW. What is he? Running around in the dessert somewhere? Did they have him?"

In the days that followed, her emotions would swing from anger to rage to disappointment and sadness, to disbelief and despair. More than once she woke up wearing one of Steve's flight suits. To cling to anything of his was therapeutic. The days ran together.

Some thought Steve had ejected and was still evading capture in the desert, not knowing that the war was over. Others thought he had been captured and not released. Maybe he had been captured and then killed? Speculation raged in the face of no new information, but there was a lot of work going on back in the desert to find answers.

The Panthers Head Home

The end of offensive air operations brought news that many had waited months to hear. It was time to go home. As one of the first units to deploy to the desert, under General Schwarzkopf's policy, the Panthers would be one of the first units to return home. But something was missing.

Someone was not coming home. Colonel Sandy Sharpe, who had led the first leg of his wing's deployment from Myrtle Beach, would not be leading his wing home. He would stay behind to make sure that everything humanly possible was done to find out what happened to Syph. His sense of duty as commander knew no other way.

Discovery

After the word got out that Syph and Sweetness had been shot down, everyone at King Fahd thought both had ejected. When the POWs were released and Steve was not one of them, the search for answers intensified. The Panthers started calling around to every Air Force Air Liaison Officer (ALO) embedded with an Army unit to be on the lookout for aircraft wreckage.

On March 22, reports came out of an Army unit bivouacked in the northwest corner of Kuwait. The unit was scouting out the terrain around their encampment when a patrolling soldier reported a crater just outside of the camp. He summoned others, who after looking at the charred sand and twisted debris, thought it might be the remains of an aircraft.

An ALO embedded with an armored unit of the 24th Infantry Division was alerted to the crash site and tentatively identified the wreckage as that of an A-10, but it was hard to tell for sure. He immediately sent word up through Air Force channels.

Early the next morning, Captain Tim Saffold, an A-10 pilot from Alex stationed at King Fahd, got a call from his squadron commander. Tim's training as an LSO, and experience as a graduate of the Air Force Accident Investigation Course, made him the perfect candidate to investigate reports that an A-10 crash site had been found. As a former ALO, he also knew how to talk to the guys on the ground.

Tim was first told he was headed north to investigate a crash site, and to "pack some gear." Colonel Tom Lyons, an Alex pilot serving as director of operations at King Fahd, joined him on the C-21 flight from King Fahd to Kuwait City. There, they would link up with an Army security detail, then board an Army Blackhawk helicopter for the twenty-minute ride to the site.

Tim was able to positively identify the wreckage as an A-10 but needed help analyzing the small pieces scattered across the desert. Tim flew south to KKMC, met up with an Army Mortuary Affairs team, and was taken to back to the site in an Army Blackhawk helicopter. After giving the pilot coordinates, he again heard, "You may have to stay out overnight." They flew over the site, then landed nearby and shut down the helo to begin the grim task of looking for identifying aircraft parts and human remains.

The crash site was nothing but a collection of small pieces and parts, which had been run over by heavy armor several times. First by the Iraqis fleeing the scene, then by the U.S. Army in hot pursuit. The team started gathering up the evidence.

They collected pieces of an aircraft engine, zippers from a G suit, twisted metal marked with part numbers, remnants of a parachute, and several bent U.S. coins. No part larger than three feet across. The team moved to the center of the crash site and was able to make out pieces of an ejection seat still in the crater. They scoured the area and collected small fragments that looked like pieces of bone. After a thorough search, they could find no other human remains.

The chopper pilot, a crusty old Warrant Officer, walked around the wreckage to see for himself. As the team was finishing up they heard, "My God." They looked over and watched as the pilot fell to his knees and started crying. Composing himself, he called out, "He gave so much."

The pilot got up, dusted himself off, and walked back to the Blackhawk. He waited for Tim and his team to complete their work, then took them back to KKMC.

Five Nickels

The investigation team assembled the small pieces collected. One of the aircraft parts was identified as a missile rail from an A-10, and it contained a serial number. The number matched a rail from tail number 78-0722, Hendo's jet. They were looking at an airplane part from Enfield 3-7.

The sight of an ejection seat in the crater meant the aircraft impacted the ground with its occupant still inside, but there were no identifiable remains. The force of the impact and fury of the explosion destroyed most everything. The sand around the impact was as hard as concrete, and from the looks of it, the Warthog was heading straight down when it hit the ground at high speed.

Back at KKMC, the mortuary affairs team was able to identify some of the material recovered as bone fragments. Small bone fragments. Twenty-five grams to be exact, the weight of five nickels.

The News

Someone came to the house and told Sharon that Steve's plane had been found. They were waiting on a positive identification to be sure. She was told the seat was still in the plane, so they were assuming he was dead.

News of the discovery of bone fragments quickly made its way to Bud and Diane Phillis. If these fragments were to be identified, however, a DNA test would be required. Bud and Diane readily agreed to provide the necessary samples to the identification team.

Samples taken, the identification team went to work. The pathology report was then completed and, at his request, reviewed by Dr. Phillis. The DNA testing results positively identified the bone fragments recovered. The agony of not knowing was replaced by the agony of knowing. Captain Stephen Richard Phillis, age thirty, of Rock Island, Illinois, was dead.

PART 11

The Real Story

Hands Full

Fresh off his final radio call of the day, Steve had his hands full. Fires continued to burn in both engines. The heat, while helping to propel Steve's A-10 onward, was causing structural damage to the tail assembly. To make matters worse, the black smoke now pouring out of each nacelle was getting thicker, making him easier to see from the ground.

Steve quickly went through the BEFORE EJECTION checklist. He looked around the cockpit and stowed all his loose items. He gathered all his classified materials and stuffed them into his flight suit. He tightened his oxygen mask, lowered his helmet visor, and tightened his chinstrap. He pulled his lap belt tight, then returned to his flying duties.

The aircraft was flying pretty well considering the damage sustained. Steve managed to get a full fifteen miles away from the site of Rob's ejection and was on course to KKMC. He was still over 130 miles away, which would take every bit of twenty-five minutes. Steve was not sure his Warthog could make it that far, but he was determined to try.

Out of the Frying Pan

Steve's egress to the southwest carried him away from the Medina but straight toward another elite Republican Guards unit, the Tawakalna Division. Positioned just outside of the northwest corner of Kuwait, they too were well-equipped, experienced, and dug in. Like the Medina, they had maintained a higher combat effectiveness than units closer to the Saudi border and were armed with the same air defense systems.

The Tawakalna knew the A-10 all too well. The prior week, King Fahd had launched thirty-two Warthogs in eight-ship formations over the course of an hour in a concentrated attack against them. The Division was six miles long and three miles wide, so the attacking force divided the target into quarters. Once overhead, the Warthogs executed coordinated attacks, releasing forty-eight high-explosive bombs within a three-minute span. The attack made everyone run for cover, and there was almost no resistance offered. Today would be different.

The inferno behind Steve was propelling him onward, but also slowly destroying both engines. Pieces and parts were falling off his airplane as it limped south. To keep his speed up, he started a shallow descent, with the black smoke pouring out of his engines still thickening. Three hundred knots was everything he could get, but it was not fast enough to escape another missile.

Back on the ground, a Tawakalna soldier spotted a black smoke trail to the north tracking south. As it inched closer, he was able to make out the shape of a Silent Gun. At first, he looked for signs of others, but once he could see that the aircraft was alone, he raced to the center of the encampment to alert his superiors.

Moments later, a Tawakalna SA-13 battery sprang to life. The commander ordered the gunner to spin the turret in the direction of the black smoke trail plainly in sight, directly overhead. It would be an easy shot.

Into the Fire

The fire control system quickly came to life, and the gunner located the target in the coarse sight in short order. He moved to the crosshairs, selected boresight, and had the missile tracking seconds later. Certain he was in range, he called "target captured" and awaited orders. "Fire!" came across the intercom, so he pressed and held down the button under his right thumb.

The missile left with a flourish of heat, noise, and smoke, and flew true to Hendo's jet. The contact fuse detonated the high-explosive warhead just aft of the flaming engines, knocking the tail clean off.

Aerodynamic forces from the wing pitched the nose down violently, generating an instantaneous negative four Gs. Steve was thrown up from the seat so hard his head hit the canopy. So violent was the force of the blow that Steve never felt a thing. Awake one second, asleep the next.

The remnants of his doomed Warthog cartwheeled to the desert below and hit the ground in a near-vertical position. The sand was hard as concrete, so the impact reduced everything to tiny little pieces. After a few minutes, the dust settled, leaving behind the scattered remains of Enfield 3-7.

Goodbyes

Celebrations of Steve's life started on April 18 in Rock Island with a private prayer service for one hundred people at Hodgson Funeral Home, followed by a funeral at St. Pius X Catholic Church. Father Mirabelli, who was supposed to preside over Steve and Sharon's wedding, had a more somber task instead.

Father Mirabelli recounted some of his memories of Steve from high school, calling him "a warm, loving, compassionate young man. He was a gentle person, always trying to make people happy." He continued:

*He died at peace with Christ, fighting for his country and what he
believed...willing to give the most precious thing he had. He gave
his life. We ask why, why one so young, so full of life, so promising...
why would God allow such a thing? And from the depths of our
hearts we cry out, hoping for some answer. He indeed stood tall, he
stood brave, and he stood with pride. He is the living flame that will
never die. He is part of the greatest realization of what America
stands for."*

The funeral card handed out before the mass read: In loving
memory of Captain Steven R. Phillis, son of Richard L. and Diane
Phillis. Inside was the Helen Steiner Rice poem "When I Must
Leave You," which talks about gallantly living on, not being afraid
to die, and watching your loved ones from the sky.

After the mass came the burial at Rock Island Memorial Park
Cemetery. It was a dreary day, made drearier by rain and thunderstorms. The ceremony was to include an A-10 flyby, but it looked
like the weather would interfere with those plans.

The forecast was for rain all day, but right before the A-10
flyby, the skies cleared up. Four Warthogs flew by and executed
a "missing man" formation. At that moment, a single bolt of
lightning struck nearby, followed by silence. Rain started to fall
again, joining the tears—and there was a downpour for the rest
of the day.

A similar scene played out at the Beach twelve days later.
Family and friends gathered at the base chapel on another dark
and stormy day for a memorial service. An artist's rendering
of Steve in his flight suit, helmet in hand, an A-10 in the back-
ground, and a map of Kuwait as the backdrop, was displayed in
the front of the chapel. A helmet and pair of gloves were placed
next to the drawing.

Thunderstorms raged outside as mourners shuffled in for the
service. After songs and scriptures, Hendo came forward to share

his memories of Steve, assisted by three visual aids—a samurai scarf, a pointer, and a teddy bear.

The samurai scarf was well-known to those who knew Steve best, as he sometimes tied it around his head, Ninja Turtle style. It stood for the spirited and fun-loving nature Steve often showed. The pointer was used while teaching, which Steve loved to do. It also represented his penchant for playing by the book. Max, Steve's big brown teddy bear, symbolized how loving, caring, and thoughtful Steve was.

Hendo said his best memories of Steve were his ability to quote Air Force regulations, his rebellious nature, and affinity for a shared bottle of good Scotch. He closed by reflecting on the last act of Steve's life, saying, "Giving his life to assist a wingman in trouble during the battle over Kuwait is the best example of the kind of man Phillis was."

Sandy Sharpe then had a powerful message for all in attendance.

We are here today to remember Captain Steven Phillis. We are here today to pay tribute to an American patriot. We are here today to burn into our memories the cost of freedom. To some, absolutely nothing is worth dying for. The truth, however, much is worth taking the risk of dying for. Men of courage have taken such risk in many worthy causes throughout our history as a free nation. Steve Phillis took such risks because Steve Phillis was truly a man of courage.

We know this not because he gave his life in the Persian Gulf, but because of the life he led in preparation for that hour. Captain Phillis was a man of excellence. Excellence as a son, a brother, a chosen partner for life. Excellence as a friend and brother fighter pilot.

But he did not achieve excellence for the recognition he would receive and so richly deserve, but because of the inner drive he felt to do so. Steve always reminded me of the words of Thoreau:

If a man does not keep pace with his companions, perhaps it is because he hears a different drummer. Let him step to the music he hears, however measured or far away.

That was Steve. A man of conviction, and a man with the courage of his own convictions. He could always see the right path, the just path, the worthy path. For him that path was service to his country through selfless dedication to his chosen profession of flying.

We are here today to burn into our memories the cost of freedom, but we also must burn into our memories the essence of courage Steve has so vividly shown us. The true meaning of excellence, of courage and conviction, and the inner feeling of fulfillment when he had truly gained the deep love of family, and the great respect of those around him. That's what I'll remember when I think of Steve, and I hope all of us here today will do the same.

Burn into our memories these cherished ideals. Maintain the courage to give our all for certain goals, whether it be flying, as was his passion, or in any other worthy walk of life.

It's easy to say that a brave man did not die in vain. That his life was lost and that it was not worthless. It is tough to truly internalize the value of his courage in our own minds.

But this is exactly what we must do. Exactly why we are here today. To remember. To grow in excellence. In that way, this memorial, it is not an ending but a beginning and a continuum for us and our chosen profession of military aviation.

Steve's wing commander ended his remarks by reciting this poem written by the wife of a fallen World War II pilot:

I knew that someday he would fly.
I saw the triumph in his eye
When, on his very first birthday
He poises, arms lifted, searched the way
From couch to chair—

Then back to there.
He did not seem to walk, he flew
Those baby steps as if he knew
He could not wait the usual way,
He must begin that very day
To climb up high,
He had to fly!
He's flying now. He has his wings
Tho' they're not man-made things
He has another pair, bomb-proof—
His soul's been growing them since youth.
I've watched them grow
For years, you know
Not feathered like the cherubim,
But, oh, so much a part of him!
Not life nor death can stop his flight,
His soul has wings into the night.
Through dark—to dawn—He shall fly on!

Sharon could still not believe he was gone. Having now watched two memorials and a "missing man" flyby, she was beginning to get the closure many prayed she would. After the service, Hendo gave Max back to Sharon, and she holds on to him to this day.

What Would You Say?

On the day after Steve's funeral, Bill Wundram wrote an article titled "What would Steve Phillis say to you, American Flag?" in the *Quad-City Times*, excerpts of which help tell the full story of our loss.

Two months ago he died for you-American Flag-and it was draped over his casket yesterday at St. Pius Church and at Hodgson Funeral, Rock Island. What would Capt. Steve Phillis, hero of the Gulf War who died to save a comrade, say to you, American Flag?

"It's red for love, and its white for peace,
and blue for the hope of free men."

—GARRISON KEILLOR

What would Steve Phillis say to you, American Flag? Always, the American Flag, for the military in times of sunshine and shadow. The American Flag's on the hearse at funeral home... The kids from Jordan School where you were a student, standing on the sidewalk as the funeral turned into the church. Ricky Coppula, a fourth grader, standing ramrod straight, holding his own American Flag. What would Steve Phillis say to you, American Flag?

Upon your stripes are written the rights of liberty and justice. The flag on your casket, so perfectly straight - like a formation of your A-10 warplanes. There are red, white and blue ribbons in the flowers around your hero's casket, but the flag itself - so big, so proud - circumscribes all that is around it... The blue field of stars, properly at the upper left hand corner of the casket, the mourners at the church sing "God Bless America," a bittersweet recessional. The flag outside is at half staff. What would Steve Phillis say to you, American Flag?

"The cross, the flag, are the embodiment of our ideals
and teach us not only how to live, but to die."

—GENERAL DOUGLAS MCARTHUR

The cemetery is grim and sodden, and the relatives cluster in the despair of a moment such as this. The flag is still there, on the casket soon to be lowered into the earth that is dark and cold. Air Force non-coms, smart in their white berets, step forward. They remove the flag. The gray casket is now bare. The flag is in the hands of the solemn Air Force people. Gently, they stretch the flag outright, and then fold it once, and then twice. Every motion is like precise puppetry. They fold it, turn it, fold it again and again until the big American Flag is compressed into a 16-inch triangle.

They release it to Lt. General Thomas Baker, Vice Commander of the Tactical Air Command of the U.S. Air Force. He is a major staff officer for the Air Force, offering tribute to a hero who has just been posthumously awarded the nation's second highest medal, the Silver Star. The General quietly speaks a few words, placing the flag into the hands of Capt. Steve's mom. She is a gentle, composed woman, resigned to the moment. She whispers her thanks. Her husband, a Rock Island physician, nods and his lips make the motion of a silent "thank you."

At the moment, as if precisely released from the heavens by the angels themselves, four desert-camouflaged A-10 war planes - the same type airship that Captain Steve Phillis flew - swoop over the grave site. The rains abruptly stop as all eyes turn to the skies and one of the planes disappears in a sweeping "arc to nowhere" in the "missing man" formation. There is not a dry eye in sight. The tears mist in a Colonel's eyes. It is one of the poignant moments of life and death in the Quad-Cities.

The American Flag is now tucked into a polished, triangular wooden box. What would Steve Phillis say to you, American Flag?

And so it is all over. The family and mourners have left, but wait, there is still another moment. While the news photographers linger on the hillside, packing up their gear, a fellow in a white Honda and wearing a blue golf coat drives up to the grave site where cemetery attendants are about to lower the casket.

He removes from his wrist a bracelet, one of those remembrances of Gulf airman missing in action.

"Do you mind?" He asks the cemetery attendants. They shrug. Into the dark hole, along with the casket, he tosses the bracelet.

One wonders what Steve Phillis would say?

A Grateful Nation

Two days after the discovery of the wreckage of Enfield 3-7, General Horner penned a letter to Steve's parents.

I have received your address from a close friend
in Davenport, Joe Krinwel, Jr. My aid, Major Marke
Gibson served with Steve in Korea and talked
with him during one of my visits to King Fahd Air
Base, just prior to 17 January. I didn't have any
special information about the shoot down or events
thereafter—I wish that I did so that I could share
them with you.

I can tell you, as you already know, your son was
indeed a very special person, as a fighter pilot,
an officer in the service of our country and as
a man. I went through a similar trial in that my
only son flies A-10s and wanted very much to be
here in the war. As a military person I understand
his duties and agreed with them. As a father, I
wanted him as far from harms way as possible.
I put my trust in God and was prepared for any
eventuality, but when I sent the guys on their
missions, each one was my son.

I wish I had the means to ease your sense of loss.
I will pray for Steve, but since I cannot, I will
make sure I maintain a special closeness to my son
and all my family. To the guys in the squadron,
Steve was a role model and now a hero—to you and
me, he was a son. May God bless you.

Chuck Horner

On April 16, Steve was awarded the Silver Star. The citation
read as follows:

Captain Stephen R. Phillis distinguished himself by gallantry in
connection with military operations against an armed enemy of
the United States during Operation Desert Storm on 15 February
1991. On that date, Captain Phillis was leading a two-ship of A-10
aircraft performing battlefield air interdiction against the Iraqi
Republican Guards Elite Medinah Armored division just north of

the northwestern border of Kuwait when wingman was shot down by a surface-to-air missile. In the face of heavy enemy anti-aircraft artillery and surface-to-air missile fire, and without regard to his personal safety, Capt. Phillis protected his downed wingman and began to coordinate search and rescue efforts. While engaged in the search and rescue coordination, he made the ultimate sacrifice while rendering aid to his fellow airman. The professional competence, aerial skill, and devotion to duty displayed by Captain Phillis in dedication of the service to his country reflect great credit upon himself and the United States Air Force.

Less than a week later, Congressman Lane Evans of Rock Island, Illinois rose before the United States House of Representatives and gave a salute to an American hero.

Time and time throughout our history, our country's armed force personnel have responded to our country's call and performed bravery in protecting our freedoms. Some have gone beyond that in sacrificing themselves and giving, as Lincoln said, their last full measure of devotion to our nation.

I rise today to salute such an American hero, Captain Steven Phillis of the USAF as one of those who gave his all to our country. While flying a mission over northwest Kuwait, Captain Phillis's A-10 warplane was shot down as he was protecting his parachuting wingman from enemy fire. According to military officials, Captain Phillis flew through thick fire to make sure his wingman, whose own plane had been hit, landed in a safe area. As his comrade was parachuting to safety, Captain Phillis continued to fly cover for him by firing at enemy ground targets.

During Operation Desert Storm, Captain Phillis also earned four air medals. My brother, who has known Captain Phillis from the time they were in grade school together, said that as long as he remembered, Steven Phillis wanted to be an air force pilot, and what pilot he was.

Captain Phillis's strength, I believe, came mostly from his family who instilled in him the values that he had upheld in combat. I know those values are also shared by his brother, Michael, who also served us well in the Gulf serving with the Navy Seabees.

I know that all my colleagues join in expressing our deepest sympathy to the Phillis family. America is America only because of the dedication of people like Captain Steven Phillis. Every freedom, every value we cherish, I believe we owe to such people as Captain Phillis and the other Americans who protected us and died in the Persian Gulf.

The final words from a grateful nation came from President Bush in a letter from the White House dated May 13, 1991.

Dear Mr. and Mrs. Phillis:

Barbara and I were deeply saddened by the news of the loss of your son, Captain Steven R. Phillis, USAF. Our hearts—indeed, the hearts of all Americans—go out to you at this very difficult time.

I understand the enormity of your grief and know that words alone could not adequately convey our sympathy. Although the days ahead will not be easy for you and your family, I hope you will take comfort in knowing that Steven served his country with courage, honor, and pride. You and your family can always be proud of him.

Although it may be of little comfort to you and your family now, history will show that Steven gave his life for his country in an important and noble cause. He served his country as a valued member of our armed forces, participating in Operation Desert Storm, not only to help liberate the innocent people of Kuwait, but also to insure that world peace has a better chance now that this naked aggression has been defeated.

He has earned our lasting respect and gratitude,
and he will be remembered for his selflessness and
sacrifice. The entire Bush family is keeping you
in its thoughts and prayers.

God Bless you.

Sincerely,
George Bush

It was particularly fitting that a man so admired by Steve delivered these words. From his commencement address at Steve's Academy graduation to his leadership during the Gulf War, President Bush was the right man at the right time. The fact he was a combat fighter pilot made these words mean even more.

We Will Miss You, Buddy!

Fighter pilots don't really know how to say goodbye to friends lost. We remember the good times, drink a toast, then get back to the dangerous work we do. Thinking too much about the past takes away from being ready for the present and future, and the world does not afford us that luxury.

Every fighter pilot who knew Steve said goodbye in his own way. Some wrote letters to the Phillis family.

From the instructors of the A-10 Fighter Weapons School:

Dear Phillis Family: We will miss Steve with you.
I hope some comfort comes in knowing that he will
be with us. He will be in the heart and mind of
every young fighter pilot who aspires to his character. He will be known to every Fighter Weapons
School graduate who feels his commitment and
his feisty energy. Trust that the school will be
better off for Steve Phillis' life. We thank you
for that, and admire your strength. God Bless you.

Captain Tom "T.J." Plutt wrote this to Steve's parents:

It is very difficult to put into words my feelings about the loss of one of my best friends and
I, a father of a 5-year old who wants to grow and
become a fighter pilot, can only wonder how you
must feel. I almost feel compelled to tell you how
Steve touched my life. "Touched" is probably an
understatement. Steve never touched a thing, he
let it have both barrels!

Steve was always there in the true spirit of
friendship. He was sincere, down to earth, hard
working, and most of all the epitome of a true
patriot.

For the past 40 days, I have waited with much hope
that things work out and I refuse to give up hope.
In the 16 years I have been associated with the
Air Force, I have yet to meet a person with as
much to give as did Steve.

I will never forget when my wife, and at the time
my 2-1/2 year-old came to visit. I left my son
with Steve as my wife and I went to get dinner. We
came back, found my boy in a pair of boxer shorts
held up with a pin boasting of being a fighter
pilot! Life has not been the same since. Another
life touched.

My heart goes out to you and all those who have
had the pleasure of knowing Steve. His loss will
be surely not forgotten by myself and Steve's
friends.

Captain Steve "Guido" Alderman wrote to Steve's family:

I flew some of my first sorties in Korea with
Steve. Despite my seven years in the Warthog, he

taught me there was still much to learn...and that
he was the best one to teach me. He taught me how
to harmonize on the best fighter pilot songs, how
to buy a great stereo system, and reminded me how
wonderful 12-year old scotch is when shared with a
friend.

Captain Tim McDonald wrote to Doctor and Mrs. Phillis:

I also learned a lot about myself with Steve.
During that first year as an A-10 pilot, I wasn't
particularly happy with my job. I very much
wanted to be assigned to an F-15 or 16 after pilot
training, and I didn't hide my disappointment very
well at Suwon. He was quick to pick up on this,
and, being intensely proud of the A-10, wasn't
real impressed with my attitude. I came to regard
my relationship with Steve as a case of being
complete opposites—we were like night and day.

Steve's heroic actions in the Gulf have had an
enormous impact on the A-10 community. Since being
assigned to Europe, I found out just how similar
Steve and I actually were. We both came from the
same part of the country. We're both academy grads
and Daedalions, and I am on my way to the weapons
school soon.

Steve would probably be very surprised that my
opinion on the A-10 has totally reversed. Steven
and his fellow "hogdrivers" have proven that the
A-10 is a wild, awesome, fighter aircraft. I am
proud to stand among the ranks of those who fly
the A-10, and damn proud to have flown with Steve.

Now that he is gone, what poetic, bittersweet
feeling it is to be striving to follow in the
footsteps of this fighter pilot—I am sure he
would be pleased. As one of his students, I will
continue to strive not to disappoint him.

Captain Mike Roberts, an F-16 pilot shot down during Desert Storm and held as a POW, wrote about his old roommate from the Academy:

> I roomed with Steve at the academy in the spring of our freshman year and the spring of our sophomore year. I heard the news of Steve's shootdown on the night of February 23rd. That was the night when the prison on Baghdad where I was being held as a POW was bombed.
>
> After the bombs hit, the guards ran away and we were able to talk to the other POWs for the first time. I couldn't believe that both of us had gotten hit. That was also the first night I was able to talk to Rob Sweet. You would not believe the love and admiration Rob has for Steve. But then anyone who was close to Steve feels the same way. Steve was always the most unselfish and ready to go guy I have ever known.
>
> There are so many things I want to say right now, but I don't know where to begin. There are two things that stick out in my mind about Steve. Number 1, he was the loudest snorer I ever had the pleasure of rooming with, and number 2, I don't think I ever heard him complain a day or say a bad word about anyone, except for a few choice words for lawyers and Saddam Hussein (I saw Steven in Saudi in November).
>
> Steve was totally devoted to his family. I can remember how he always talked about you and his grandparents and how devastated he was when his grandfather died. He just sucked it up, held it all in, and in typical Steve Phillis fashion, turned to helping out other people with their problems.

I have read the accounts of how Steve was shot
down, and would have expected no less of him.
He was afraid of nothing and would never leave
a friend in need. Steve loved his job as all of
fighter pilots do, and I know he would not have
traded a minute of it for anything.

I found it hard to explain how I feel right now.
I thank the good Lord everyday that I was able to
return home to my wife and a son born on February
21st of this year, but at the same time find
myself questioning why Steve is not still with us.
I truly do believe, however, that Steve was met by
his grandfather on the way to heaven. I can guar-
anty that my son will hear about Steve Phillis
from the time he is old enough to listen — one of
the best men and most shit hot fighter pilots I
have ever known.

I could go on for pages and pages telling you the
good things that I remember about Steve. I just
wanted to let you know that I am one of millions
who will never forget Steve or stop appreciating
what he has done. He <u>did</u> make a difference in
helping us win that war, and he <u>did</u> make a difference in the lives of a lot of people. This may
sound corny or trite, but I know I am a better
person for having had the pleasure of rooming and
serving with Steve.

Others were more public with their thoughts. This "In Memo-
riam" was published in the U.S. Air Force Fighter Weapons
Review, summer 1991 edition, and written by Lieutenant Colonel
Brian Jones, the A-10 Division Commander. It read:

On 15 February, 1991, Captain Stephen R. Phillis
was killed in action, leading a two-ship of A-10's
in an attack on Iraqi Republican Guards forces.
His aircraft was destroyed by a surface-to-air

missile while he was escorting his battle-damaged
wingman out of target area in northwest Kuwait.
Captain Phillis was awarded the Silver Star on
30 April 1991.

The graduates of the U.S.A.F. Fighter Weapons
School express our deepest sympathy to Steve's
family and fiancé; their intense courage and
patriotism has been an inspiration for us to
carry on.

The loss of a brother is an agonizing cost for
the protection of our American ideals. But in that
loss we pledge to remember...even memorialize...
the spirit of our business. Many a budding weapons
officer will aspire to the spark, humor, drive,
flying ability, and personal loyalty of Steve
Phillis. All of our instructors will continue
to infuse that kind of character into the patch.
For it is not just our past we drink and toast to
here...it's our future. Thanks Steve.... We will
miss you, buddy!"

As for me, this book, a long time in the making, is my way of
saying goodbye. It was important to me to share Steve's story with
as many people as possible and to answer some of the questions
many of us still have.

Should I Stay or Should I Go?

The first question many people ask is, "Why didn't Steve leave
when he had the chance?" We know for certain that immediately
following Rob Sweet's ejection Steve confirmed a good chute,
contacted AWACS to start the search and rescue, and called
Pachmayr for additional support. His duties as flight lead were
complete, but his duty to Rob Sweet had just begun.

Steve felt personally responsible for Sweet's shootdown. They
could have left earlier. They could have left after the first SAM

launch. They did neither, and since it was Steve's call to make, he owned it. He was only concerned for Sweetness. Heroism never entered his mind; he was doing the job he had trained to do and was upholding the contract that he had with his wingman.

Syph lived his life by a simple code. Family, friends, faith, fiancée, and fighter pilot. His duty as fighter pilot was to his wingman. They would fly together, fight together, and God willing, return together. Steve's decision to stay was in part to honor the legacy of those before him who also put service above self. Leaving simply never crossed his mind.

Pull the Handles

The second question a few people ask is, "Why didn't he eject?" Was he afraid to pull the handles? Was he afraid of getting captured? Was he afraid that if captured he would divulge the war plans stored in his head? Did he decide to just ride it in to protect all that he knew? The notion that Steve passed up the opportunity to eject for any of these reasons is complete and utter bullshit. Here's why.

Steve was especially well-trained for ejection. It started with his first additional duty as the LSO at Alex, where he not only learned everything about the A-10's ejection system and survival equipment, but also taught others how to use them. His training and experience as a CSAR pilot at Suwon, Myrtle Beach, and KKMC only reinforces this point. Of any pilot flying the A-10 in Desert Storm, Steve would never have doubted his ability to safety eject. He was not afraid to eject and had every reason to do so if he knew his Warthog was going down.

Steve had so much to live for, starting with his family. He was extremely close to his parents, especially his mother, along with his brothers and sister. Sharon was the love of his life, and their recent engagement was a continuous source of strength and inspiration. He ended his February 15 letter to Sharon with, "I love you with all my heart and will love you forever." Every letter home was a reminder of how much he looked forward to the future, and at age thirty had everything in front of him. He would not willingly give up on any of them.

Steve was a fighter. From the Alleman High School football field to his boxing days at the Academy, through survival school, crud, and dozens of competitive Air Force training programs, he battled. The idea that he would give up in any way runs completely contrary to everything about him.

Some think he was concerned that the knowledge in his head about the upcoming ground war could be compromised. For that to even be an issue, a lot of things would have to have happened. First, he would have to be captured. Given his survival skills, and the approach of CSAR forces, that was far from certain. What is certain is the Steve would not have given up without quite a fight. If he really worried about capture, he could have saved the last round in his service revolver to finish the job. This option was expressed by more than one pilot.

Next, he would have to be turned over to skilled interrogators and tortured to a degree where he would surrender this vital information. Though we will really never know, nobody who knew him well could imagine him breaking. Indeed, his decision to stay in the target area in the face of extraordinary personal danger makes this point well.

The only answer that makes any sense is that Steve was unable to eject, and the wreckage of his A-10 proves this point. So in the end, the real reason Captain Stephen Richard Phillis remained in the target area to protect his downed wingman boils down to a single word: love.

No Greater Love

John 15:13 reads, "Greater love has no one than this, than to lay down one's life for his friends." It seems odd to attribute love to a fighter pilot, as there are so many other words to choose from. Flying and fighting seem so far away from love, yet love is the lone word that explains why Steve did what he did. Besides, it's true.

When people live together in close quarters under less-than-ideal conditions, it brings them together. When they train for a dangerous job, they get closer. When they go out together and lay their lives on the line for something they believe in, they get closer still. When they place their lives in the hands of another, like flight lead and wingman do, it creates a bond so strong few can ever really understand it.

Steve loved life, his family, Sharon, his A-10, his squadron, his country, and his wingman. That he was willing to lay his life on the line is one thing. That he paid the ultimate price for that love is another thing altogether.

Once a Hero

If the world needs a role model, then look no further than Steve Phillis. Not in it for the money, not concerned with anything other than getting the job done, Steve lived his life his way. He had nothing to prove to anyone except himself, and by setting high standards and living them, he was all he was ever going to need to be.

Glory, fame, and fortune were goals for someone else. Steve believed in his country and the responsibility he accepted as a defender of freedom. While for some there is little glory in this, to Steve it meant everything, and it was something for which he was willing to give his life.

Steve chose to fulfill this duty to his country as a warrior. He took the responsibility as part of the world's mightiest fighting force deadly seriously. To that end, he dedicated countless hours of time studying, thinking, teaching, and perfecting his craft. He set out to be the best that he possibly could, not for the sake of recognition, but to do "what ought to be done."

We need more role models like Steve Phillis: motivated by commitment, dedication, perseverance, and self-sacrifice. These are the kinds of things that we should point to and say to our children, "If you want to be like someone, be like Steve. Go where your life takes you, be happy in the journey, and be happy with both the path you take and the way you walk it. Fame and glory may be yours one day but should be a byproduct of your journey and not an end." For that lesson, we all owe Steve a debt of gratitude.

Hendo said it best, "He died doing what he thought was right. That was Steve Phillis."

MOH

Our nation's highest award for valor in action against an enemy force is the Medal of Honor. The award requires that a recipient "distinguished himself conspicuously by gallantry and intrepidity at the risk of his life above and beyond the call of duty" while engaged in military operations involving conflict with an opposing foreign force. This standard requires acts of personal bravery or self-sacrifice so conspicuous as to clearly distinguish the individual above his comrades and must have involved risk of life. How do Captain Stephen Richard Phillis's actions on February 15, 1991, stack up against this standard?

Steve was shot down and killed by Iraq's Republican Guards during a named operation. The questions, then, center around whether he (1) clearly distinguished himself conspicuously by gallantry, and (2) at the risk of his life above and beyond the call of duty.

The enemy he faced on February 15 was the Medina Division of the Republican Guards. The Medina were equipped with Iraq's most modern military weapons, well-trained to use them, and had ten years of recent combat experience against Iran. The ferocity of their resistance was revealed by the A-10s damaged earlier in the same day and by the intense anti-aircraft fire experienced by others during the ingress of Steve's flight. Nevertheless, he pressed his attack against the Medina Division.

Near the end of his successful attacks, Steve's wingman was hit and forced to eject over the enemy troops they had just finished bombing. Steve watched his wingman safely eject, noted his position, and radioed AWACS for search and rescue support. At this point, Steve had met his duty as a flight lead and had the opportunity to safety egress the target area.

Instead, he stayed behind to support his wingman, who was now floating down in a parachute into a hail of gunfire. As the only remaining A-10 over the division, he immediately drew the attention of every surface-to-air missile and anti-aircraft artillery battery by popping flares to bring help to Rob, and he would be able to clearly see the smoke, tracers, and missiles launched at him. Still he stayed. For three minutes and forty-five seconds, an eternity over a target complex, with complete disregard for his personal safety, he stayed to help his wingman.

In a last act of heroism in the face of grave personal danger, he keyed the microphone, and using the code word for aircraft down, called "Enfield 3-7 is bag as well." Steve was awarded the Silver Star for his bravery, but what does it take for a fighter pilot to earn the Medal of Honor?

Fighter pilots have earned the Medal of Honor in a variety of ways, as these examples illustrate. Captain Lance Sijan, the Air Force Academy graduate mentioned by Vice President Bush during Steve's commencement speech, courageously resisted his North Vietnamese captors, escaped once, and endured extreme torture without divulging any information of military value. World War II P-51 Pilot Lieutenant Colonel James Howard, while separated from his flight, single-handedly protected a bomber formation by attacking thirty enemy fighters in complete disregard for his own safety. Lieutenant Colonel Leo Thorsness, piloting an F-105 over North Vietnam, repeatedly risked his life to save a downed aircrew from capture while assisting the search and rescue effort. Colonel William A. Jones III was flying an A-1H Skyraider over North Vietnam in 1968 as an on-scene commander in an attempted rescue of a downed pilot. He was repeatedly hit by anti-aircraft fire but continued the search, then flew his crippled plane back to base to pass along information for the rescue before receiving medical attention.

These examples demonstrate that it is not how long the bravery lasts, but the risk in the face of danger. Steve's duty as flight lead was to confirm the safe ejection of his wingman, note his position, and begin search and rescue efforts. All that was done within a minute of Rob Sweet's ejection.

Staying almost four times longer is the definition of "gallantry above and beyond the call of duty," given the intense anti-aircraft fire, the enemy's awareness of his position, his lack of supporting aircraft, and his inability to safely escape because of his low altitude and the A-10's lack of speed. Add to that his decision to dispense high-visibility pyrotechnic flares to get the inbound A-10s "eyes on," knowing that it would attract the attention of every Iraqi soldier on the ground with a gun or missile to shoot—the definition of combat heroics.

Captain Stephen Richard Phillis's conduct in the face of mortal danger with complete disregard for his personal safety was aimed at saving another. Is this not exactly what the Medal of Honor should recognize? "What does a fighter pilot have to do to earn the Medal of Honor?"

If Steve were still with us, he would tell us no, he was just doing his job the only way he knew how. But by his sacrifice, he cannot speak, so we as a nation must speak for him. The dedication in the beginning of this book addressed to my children reads, "So that you will know a true hero when you see one."

Five Nickels Tribute

The grave of Stephen Richard Phillis lies on the west side of the Rock Island Memorial Park Cemetery, and if you ever get the chance to visit, you should go. It is worth the trip to share time with his legacy. Near his grave is a flagpole, at the base of which lies this plaque.

Remember
STEPHEN R. PHILLIS
Captain
United States Air Force

If you listen carefully, perhaps you can still hear the four A-10s that flew the "missing man" formation on that rainy day in April. Or perhaps you will catch a glimpse of a dark speck near the horizon flying home. If it is raining, surely you will feel the tears as they fall.

Before you leave, throw a nickel in the grass. Better yet, throw five. One for the family he loved. One for the woman he loved, one for the wingman he loved, one for the airplane he loved, and one for the country he loved. For no greater love....

Bibliography

Air Force Instruction 11-2A-10C, Volume 3, 2 March 2012 Incorporating Change 1, 19 August 2013, Flying Operations, A-10C – Operations Procedures. United States Air Force, 2013. www.e-publishing.af.mil. Retrieved December 17, 2019.

"Base Remembers Fallen Comrade." *Strand Century*, May 3, 1991.

Bourque, Stephen A., *JAYHAWK! The VII Corps in the Persian Gulf War* (Washington, D.C.: The Center of Military History, 2002).

Carhart, Tom, *Iron Soldiers: How America's 1st Armored Division Crushed Iraq's Elite Republican Guard* (New York: Random House, 1994).

Clancy, Tom with General Chuck Horner, *Every Man a Tiger* (New York, G.P. Putnam's Sons, 1999).

Cohen, Dr. Eliot, John Hopkins University's School of Advanced International Studies, "Gulf War Air Power Survey, Volume IV – Weapons, Tactics, and Training." Washington, D. C. 1993. Commissioned by Secretary of the Air Force Donald B. Rice.

Coyne, Kevin, "The Ejection Site: The ACES II Seat: Tech Info," www.ejectionsite.com/acesiitech.htm, Retrieved December 18, 2019.

"Depleted uranium shell: what is it and how does it work?" sodiummedia.com, 2019, en.sodiummedia.com/4075518-depleted-uranium-shell-what-is-it-and-how-does-it-work. Retrieved December 18, 2019.

Desert Storm: 30 Years Later: Lessons from the 1991 Air Campaign in the Persian Gulf War, The Mitchell Institute for Aerospace Studies (Arlington, VA.: The Air Force Association, March 2021).

Elliott, DJ, "Iraqi Security Force Order of Battle: August 2008 Update," FDD's Long War Journal, August 4, 2008. www.longwarjournal.org/archives/2008/08/iraqi_security_force_18.php. Retrieved March 1, 2021.

"GAU-8/A Avenger," National Museum of the USAF. web.archive.org/web/20100416063452/http://www.national-museum.af.mil/factsheets/factsheet.asp?id=1019. Retrieved December 18, 2019.

Glosson, General Buster, *War With Iraq: Critical Lessons* (Charlotte, NC, Glosson Family Foundation, 2003).

Hallion, Richard P., *"Storm over Iraq: Air Power and the Gulf War,"* (Washington, D.C., Smithsonian Institution Press, 1992).

Huff, Melissa and Andrew Shain, "354th Members Return from Gulf with Stories, Memories," *The Sun News*, May 5, 1991.

Kopp, Carlo, "KBTochmash 9K35 Strela-10 Self Propelled Air Defense System/SA-13 Gopher," Technical Report APA-TR-2009-0801, *Air Power Australia*, April 2012. www.ausairpower.net/APA-9K35-Strela-10.html. Retrieved January 18, 2020.

Lofton, Dewanna, "Day, Pilot's Memorial Somber," *The Sun News*, April 19, 1991.

Lowry, Richard S., *The Guld War Chronicles: A Military History of the First War with Iraq* (New York, iUniverse, 2008).

"Manual Russian 9K35M Strela-10M MT-LB Rocket System." Translated by Google Translate. Ministry of Defense of the Russian Federation, date unknown, Accessed April 29, 2020. translate.google.com/u/5/?hl=en&tab=mT.

Neff, Lisa, "Capt. Phillis Now at Final Peace," *The Daily Dispatch*, April 18, 1991.

"Northrop AT-38B Talon," National Museum of the United States Air Force, July 13, 2015. www.nationalmuseum.af.mil/Visit/ Museum-Exhibits/Fact-Sheets/Display/Article/196733/ northrop-at-38b-talon/. Retrieved April 12, 2020.

Operation Desert Storm: Evaluation of the Air Campaign, Washington D.C. Government Reprints Press 2002.

Phillis, Steven, "Have Quick II," USAF Fighter Weapons Review, Summer 1988.

Putney, Diane Therese, "Airpower Advantage: Planning the Gulf War Air Campaign, 1989–1991," Air Force History and Museums Program, United States Air Force, 2004.

"Regulations, Shooting, and Combat Work on Anti-Aircraft Missile Complexes 'Strela-10M,'" Translated by Google Translate. Ministry of Defense of the Russian Federation, date unknown. Accessed April 29, 2020. translate.google. com/u/5/?hl=en&tab=mT.

Scales, Robert H, *Certain Victory: The U.S. Army in the Gulf War* (Washington, D.C., United States Army, 1993).

Smallwood, William L., *Warthog: Flying the A-10 in the Gulf War* (Dulles, VA., Potomac Books, 1993)

"Strela-10M3 (SA-13 "Gopher") IR SAM System." Military Technology 2/93, Bad Neuenahr – Ahrweiler, Germany: Monch Publishing Group, 1993.

"T.O. 1A-10A-1 Flight Manual USAF Series A-10A Aircraft, 20 February 1983, incorporating change 8 dated 15 March 1988." United States Air Force, 1988.

"T.O. 1A-10A-34-1-1 Non-Nuclear Weapons Delivery Manual, USAF Series A-10A/OA-10A Aircraft, 3 May 1999." United States Air Force, 1999.

Thompson, Rod, "RI Pilot Died a Hero." *Quad-City Times*, April 17, 1991.

Thompson, Rod, "Tears Flow for War Hero." *Quad-City Times*, April 19, 1991.

Thompson, Rod, "Taps Sounds for War Heroes." *Quad-City Times*, May 27, 1991.

USAF Manned Aircraft Combat Losses 1990-2002, Maxwell Air Force Base, AL: Air Force Historical Research Agency, December 9, 2002.

Woods, Kevin M., "Iraqi Perspectives Project Phase II Um Al-Ma'arik (The Mother of All Battles): Operational and Strategic Insights from an Iraqi Perspective," Alexandria, VA: Institute for Defense Analyses, 2008.

"30MM GAU 8/A." General Dynamics Ordnance and Tactical Systems, General Dynamics, September 21, 2005.

Acknowledgments

Assembling the story of one man's life and heroic death has led me to incredible people eager to share the legacy of Captain Steve Phillis. To all those mentioned, and to the those inadvertently left out, a heartfelt thank you for your support.

Thanks to...

The Phillis family of Bud, Diane, Mike, Tom, Tim, and Catherine, for trusting a stranger with the inside story of your amazing Steve.

Sharon Taflan Martin for sharing the stories and hundreds of letters to and from your Steve.

Major General Sandy and Jo Sharpe, for trusting an Eagle Driver with the precious and guarded details of Steve's combat prowess and final mission.

Greg "Hendo" Henderson for the whole truth about a world class fighter pilot, and for keeping his story alive all these years.

Rob "Sweetness" Sweet for always being a great wingman to Steve.

General Chuck Horner, for insisting I stick to the facts and avoid a "fairy tale." The ultimate fighter pilot's fighter pilot.

Warthog drivers from around the world who rallied to answer my questions, track down people, and offer unwavering support for recognizing Syph's heroics, including Reptile, Gils, Chip, Hacksaw, Beave, Jewels, Mongo, KC, PJ, Ragman, BB, Whale,

Root, Boog, Fish, Danno, Danny, Boot, JD, Rick Shatzel, Buck, and countless others. A special thanks to Boot Hill for his work on "Hogs in the Sand" and for permission to share this work with others.

Lieutenant General "Orville" Wright, Major General Doug Raaberg, 14th Chief Master Sergeant of the Air Force Gerald Murray, Tobias Naegele, and Brian Everstine of the Air Force Association for helping to tell the stories of all our Airmen.

The United States Air Force Academy and the Air Force Academy Association of Graduates.

Blade Whelan, Brian Whetstone, and Eric Rubenstein from the 507 Air Defense Adversary Squadron at Nellis Air Force Base, Nevada, for the up close and personal tour of the SA-13.

Jon Land, Jeff Ayers, Dan Schilling, and Lori Chapman Longfritz for the encouragement, wisdom, and advice that helped get this book published.

Paul Jacobsmeyer from the Defense Office of Pre-Publication and Security Review, and Andrew Davis from the Air Force Book Program Manager, for helping to get the manuscript reviewed and approved for release.

Nancy Jarvi for all the transcription work early on in the project.

About the Author

Brigadier General Jim "Boots" Demarest is an author and speaker uniquely qualified to tell the story of Captain Steve Phillis. They graduated together from the Air Force Academy, after which Jim spent ten years as an F-15 fighter pilot. He was a distinguished graduate of the Fighter Weapons School "Top Gun" program, and served in Desert Storm.

Following a break in service to attend Cornell Law School and work as an attorney and professional speaker, Boots returned to military service in the Florida Air National Guard as a JAG. General Demarest was promoted into a leadership position as Chief of Staff and Deputy Commanding General, and is a sought-after speaker on topics including leadership and execution improvement.